# THE FACT-FINDERS
# UNIVERSE

DK

**Project Editors** Srijani Ganguly, Abi Maxwell
**Senior Art Editor** Nehal Verma
**US Senior Editor** Shannon Beatty
**Jacket Designer** Rashika Kachroo
**Pre-Production Designer** Bimlesh Tiwary
**Production Editor** Dragana Puvacic
**Senior Production Controller** Leanne Burke
**Managing Editor** Roohi Sehgal
**Managing Art Editors** Anna Hall, Romi Chakraborty
**Delhi Creative Head** Malavika Talukder
**Associate Publisher** Gemma Farr
**Art Director** Mabel Chan
**Associate Publishing Director** Francesca Young
**Consultants** Dr. Mike Goldsmith, Josh Barker

Created in collaboration with Raspberry Books
**Author** Tracey Turner
**Artist** Gillian Reid
**Design** Nicola Scott
**Art direction and series design** Sidonie Beresford-Browne

*For Toby, as always, remembering stargazing in Gaucín T.T.*
*For Matt, for all the shared adventures and support G.R.*

First American Edition, 2025
Published in the United States by DK Publishing,
a division of Penguin Random House LLC
1745 Broadway, 20th Floor, New York, NY 10019

Copyright © 2025 Raspberry Books Ltd
25 26 27 28 29  10 9 8 7 6 5 4 3 2 1
001–345413–Jul/2025

All rights reserved.
Without limiting the rights under the copyright reserved above, no part of this publication may be reproduced, stored in or introduced into a retrieval system, or transmitted, in any form, or by any means (electronic, mechanical, photocopying, recording, or otherwise), without the prior written permission of the copyright owner. No part of this publication may be used or reproduced in any manner for the purpose of training artificial intelligence technologies or systems.

Published in Great Britain by Dorling Kindersley Limited

ISBN: 978-0-5939-6532-0

DK books are available at special discounts when purchased in bulk for sales promotions, premiums, fund-raising, or educational use. For details, contact: DK Publishing Special Markets, 1745 Broadway, 20th Floor, New York, NY 10019
SpecialSales@dk.com

Printed and bound in China

www.dk.com

MIX
Paper | Supporting responsible forestry
FSC™ C018179

This book was made with Forest Stewardship Council™ certified paper—one small step in DK's commitment to a sustainable future. Learn more at www.dk.com/uk/information/sustainability

# THE FACT-FINDERS
# UNIVERSE

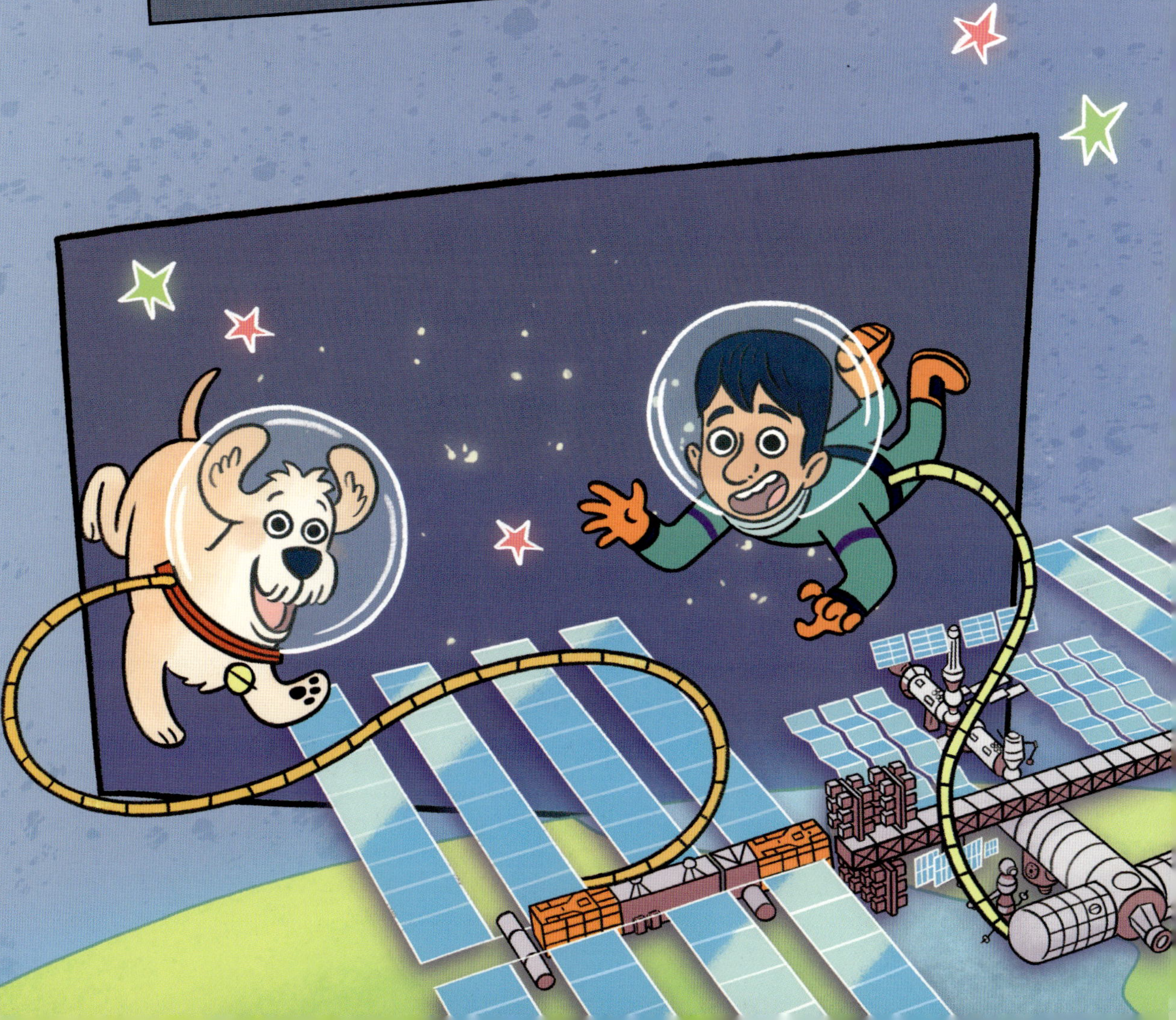

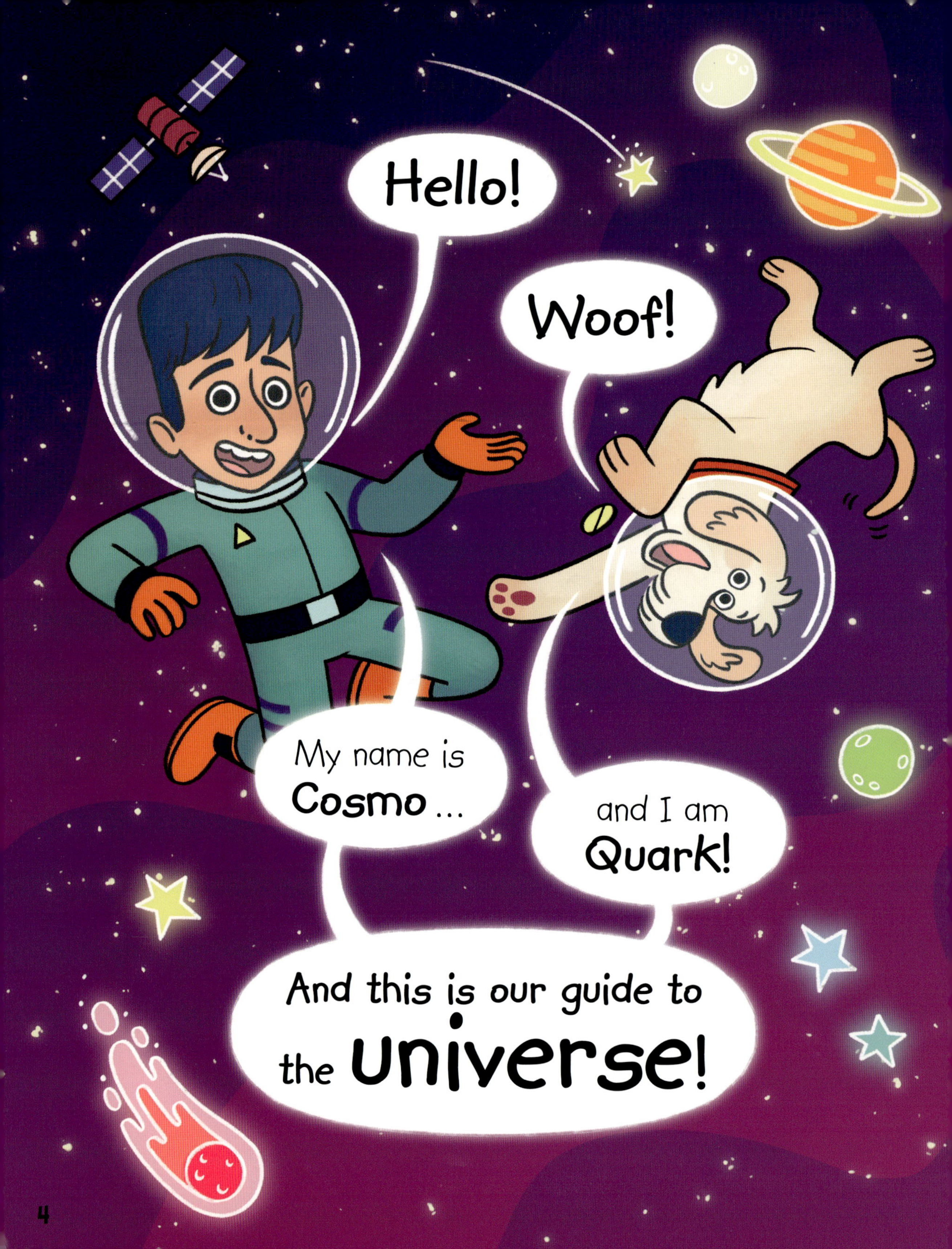
Hello!
Woof!
My name is Cosmo ...
and I am Quark!
And this is our guide to the universe!

# Find out...

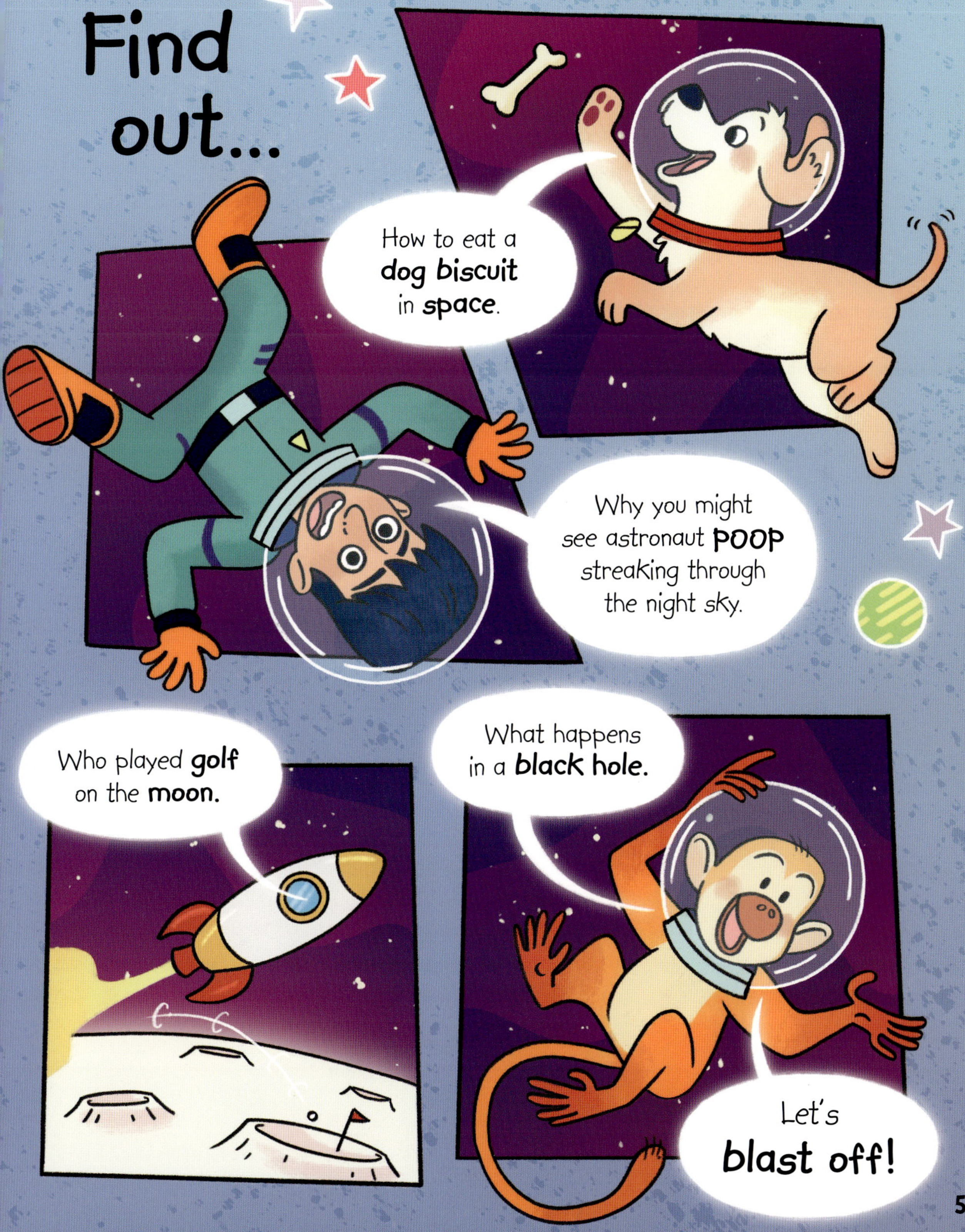
How to eat a **dog biscuit** in **space**.
Why you might see astronaut **POOP** streaking through the night sky.
Who played **golf** on the **moon**.
What happens in a **black hole**.
Let's **blast off!**

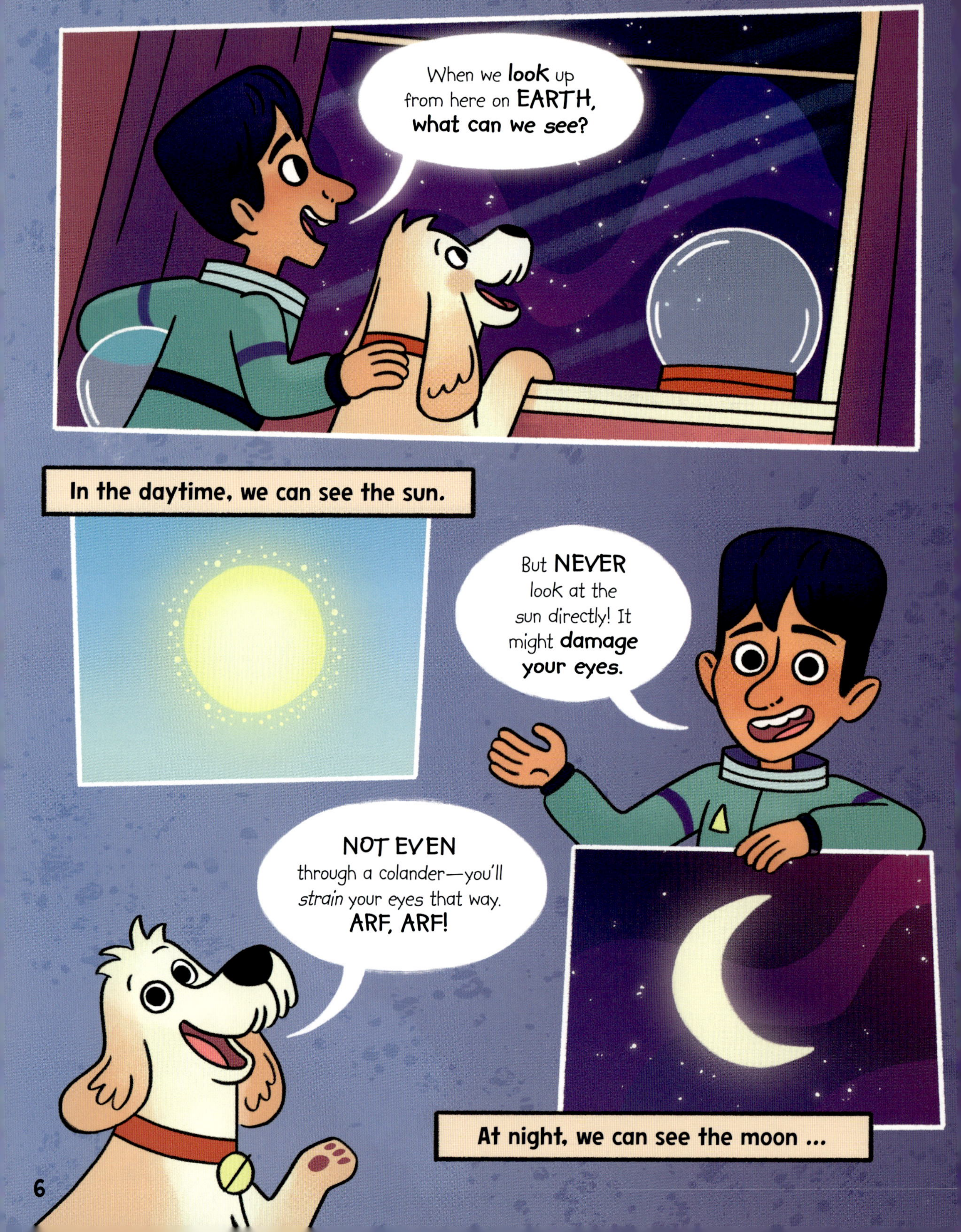
When we look up from here on EARTH, what can we see?
In the daytime, we can see the sun.
But NEVER look at the sun directly! It might damage your eyes.
NOT EVEN through a colander—you'll strain your eyes that way. ARF, ARF!
At night, we can see the moon ...

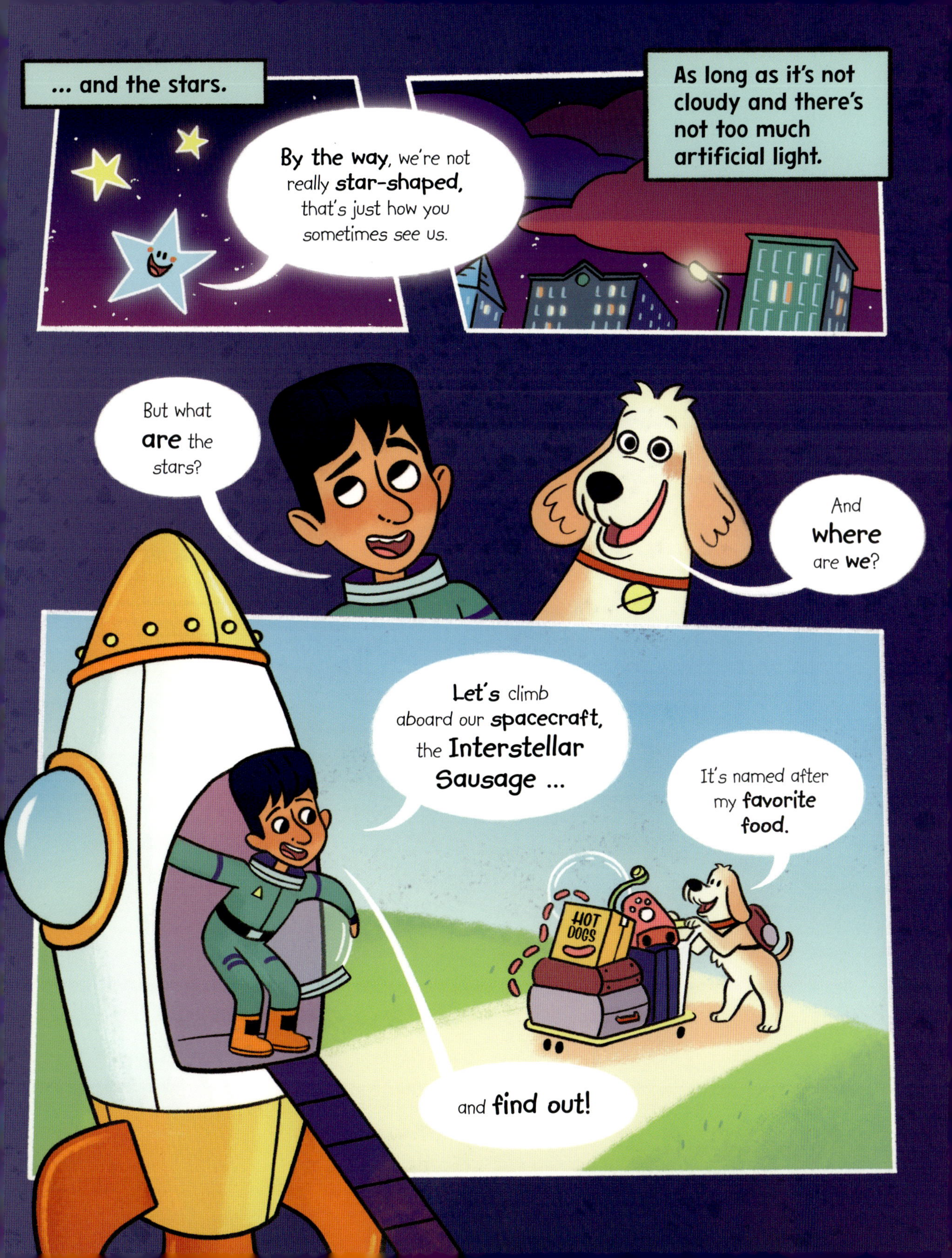
... and the stars.
By the way, we're not really star-shaped, that's just how you sometimes see us.
As long as it's not cloudy and there's not too much artificial light.
But what are the stars?
And where are we?
Let's climb aboard our spacecraft, the Interstellar Sausage ...
It's named after my favorite food.
HOT DOGS
and find out!

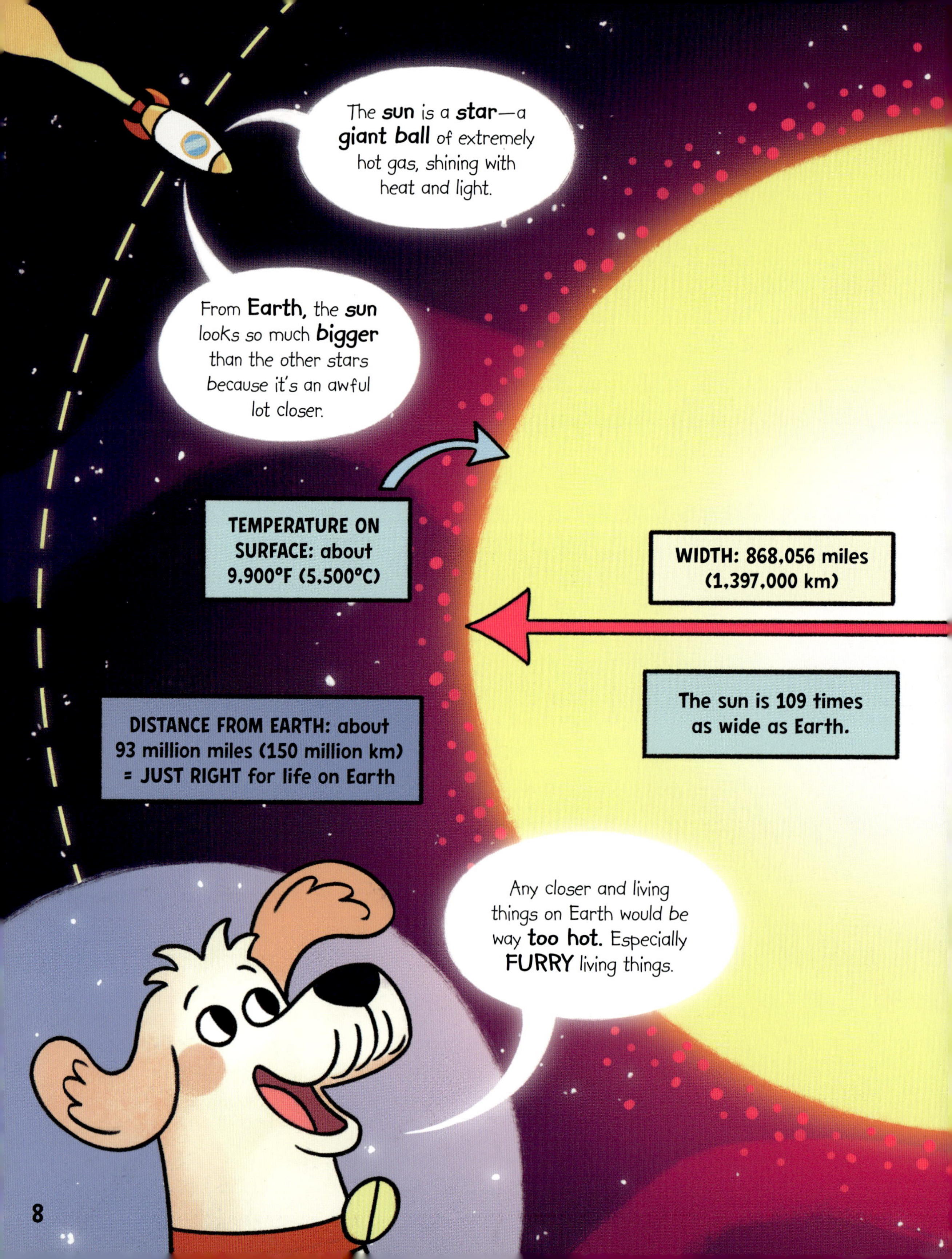
The sun is a star—a giant ball of extremely hot gas, shining with heat and light.
From Earth, the sun looks so much bigger than the other stars because it's an awful lot closer.
TEMPERATURE ON SURFACE: about 9,900°F (5,500°C)
WIDTH: 868,056 miles (1,397,000 km)
The sun is 109 times as wide as Earth.
DISTANCE FROM EARTH: about 93 million miles (150 million km) = JUST RIGHT for life on Earth
Any closer and living things on Earth would be way too hot. Especially FURRY living things.

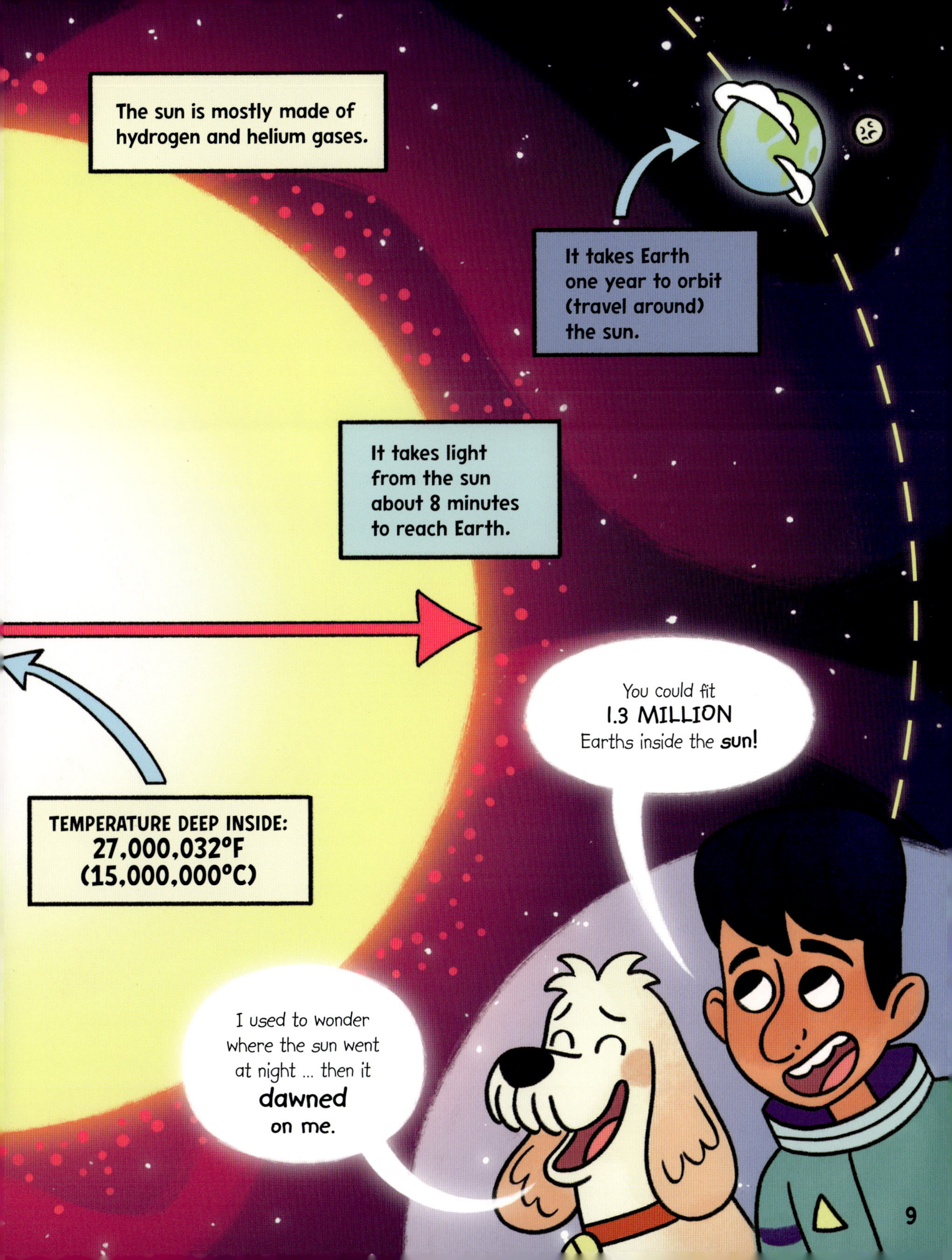

The sun is mostly made of hydrogen and helium gases.
It takes Earth one year to orbit (travel around) the sun.
It takes light from the sun about 8 minutes to reach Earth.
You could fit 1.3 MILLION Earths inside the sun!
TEMPERATURE DEEP INSIDE: 27,000,032°F (15,000,000°C)
I used to wonder where the sun went at night ... then it dawned on me.

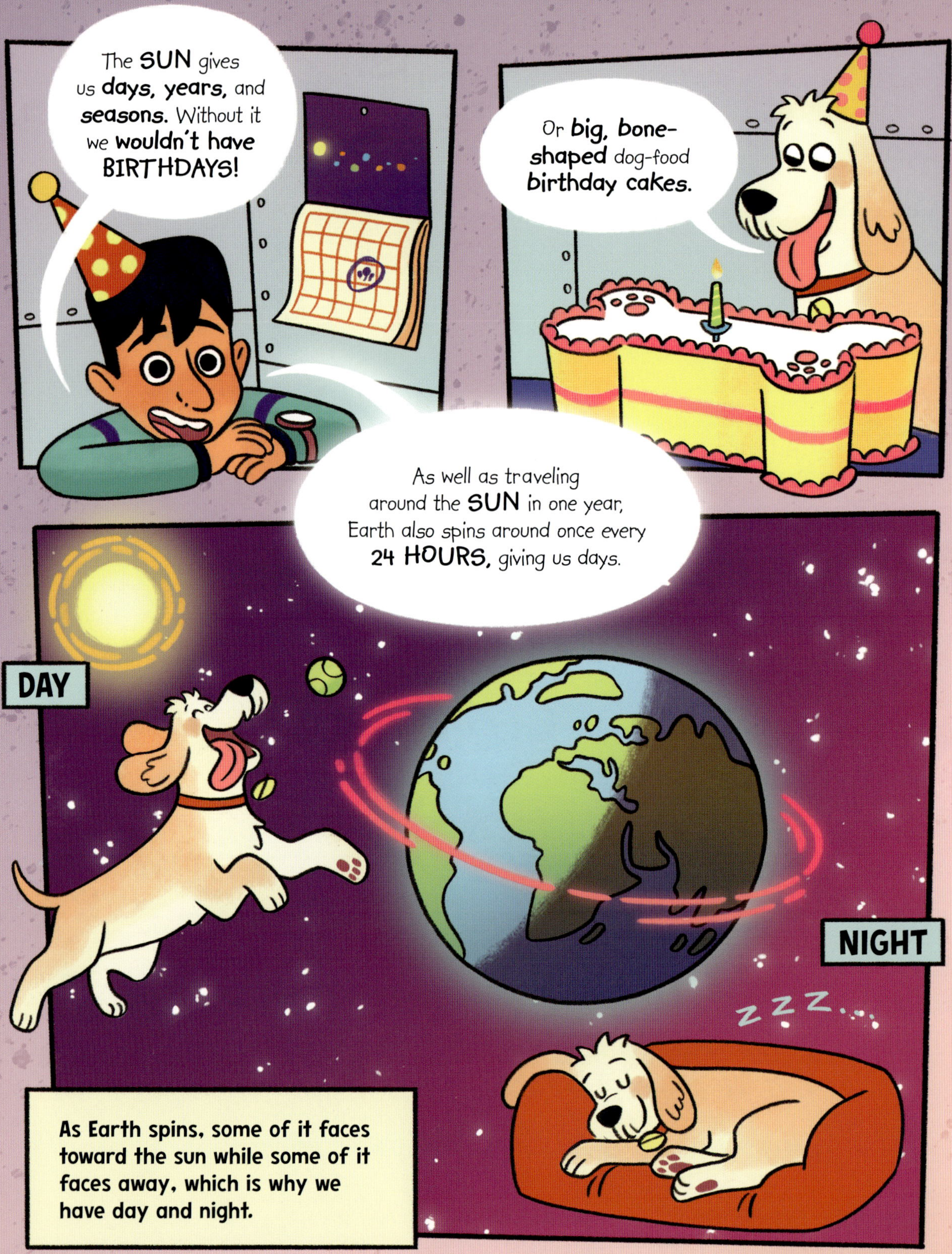

The SUN gives us days, years, and seasons. Without it we wouldn't have BIRTHDAYS!
Or big, bone-shaped dog-food birthday cakes.
As well as traveling around the SUN in one year, Earth also spins around once every 24 HOURS, giving us days.
DAY
NIGHT
ZZZ...
As Earth spins, some of it faces toward the sun while some of it faces away, which is why we have day and night.

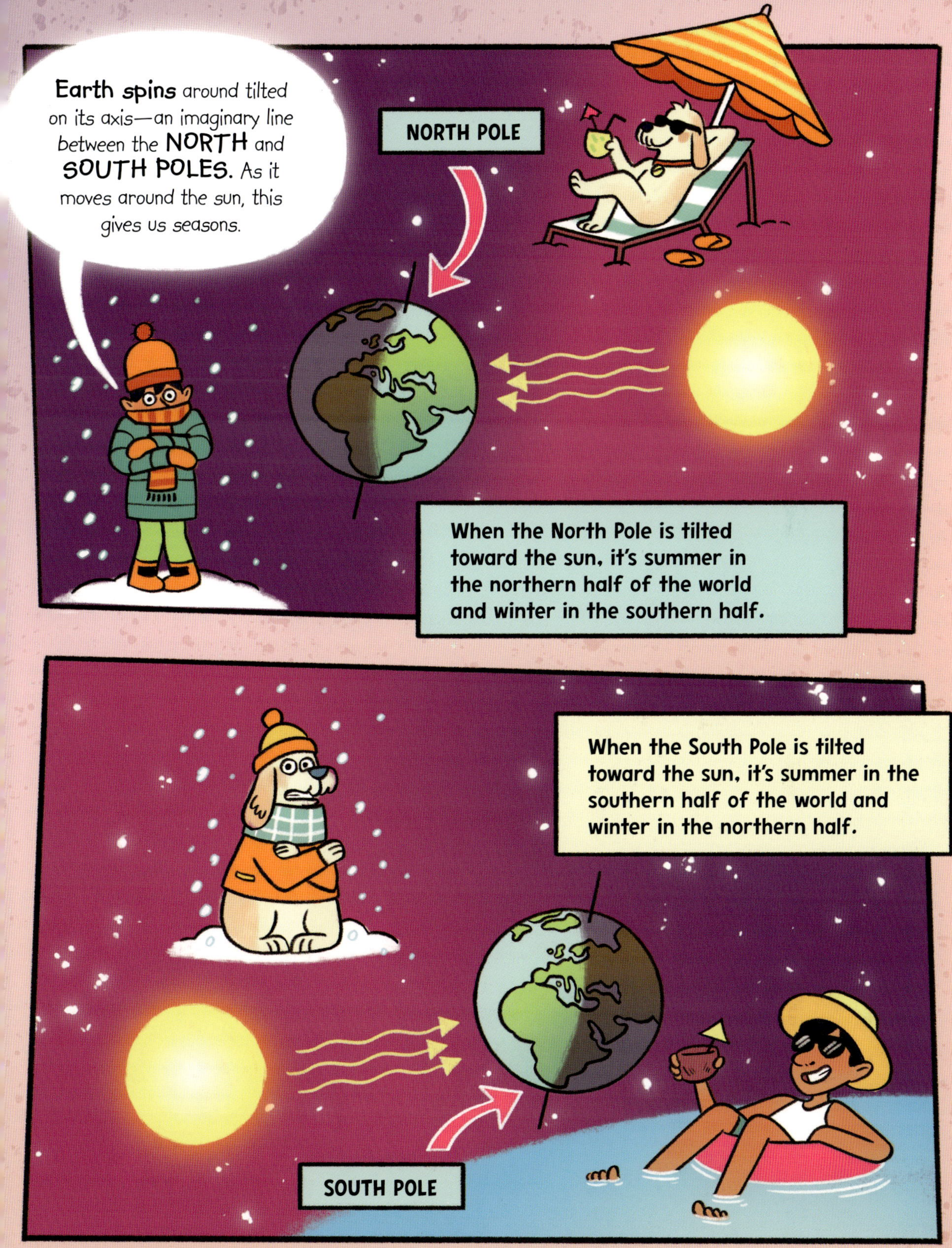
Earth spins around tilted on its axis—an imaginary line between the NORTH and SOUTH POLES. As it moves around the sun, this gives us seasons.
NORTH POLE
When the North Pole is tilted toward the sun, it's summer in the northern half of the world and winter in the southern half.
When the South Pole is tilted toward the sun, it's summer in the southern half of the world and winter in the northern half.
SOUTH POLE

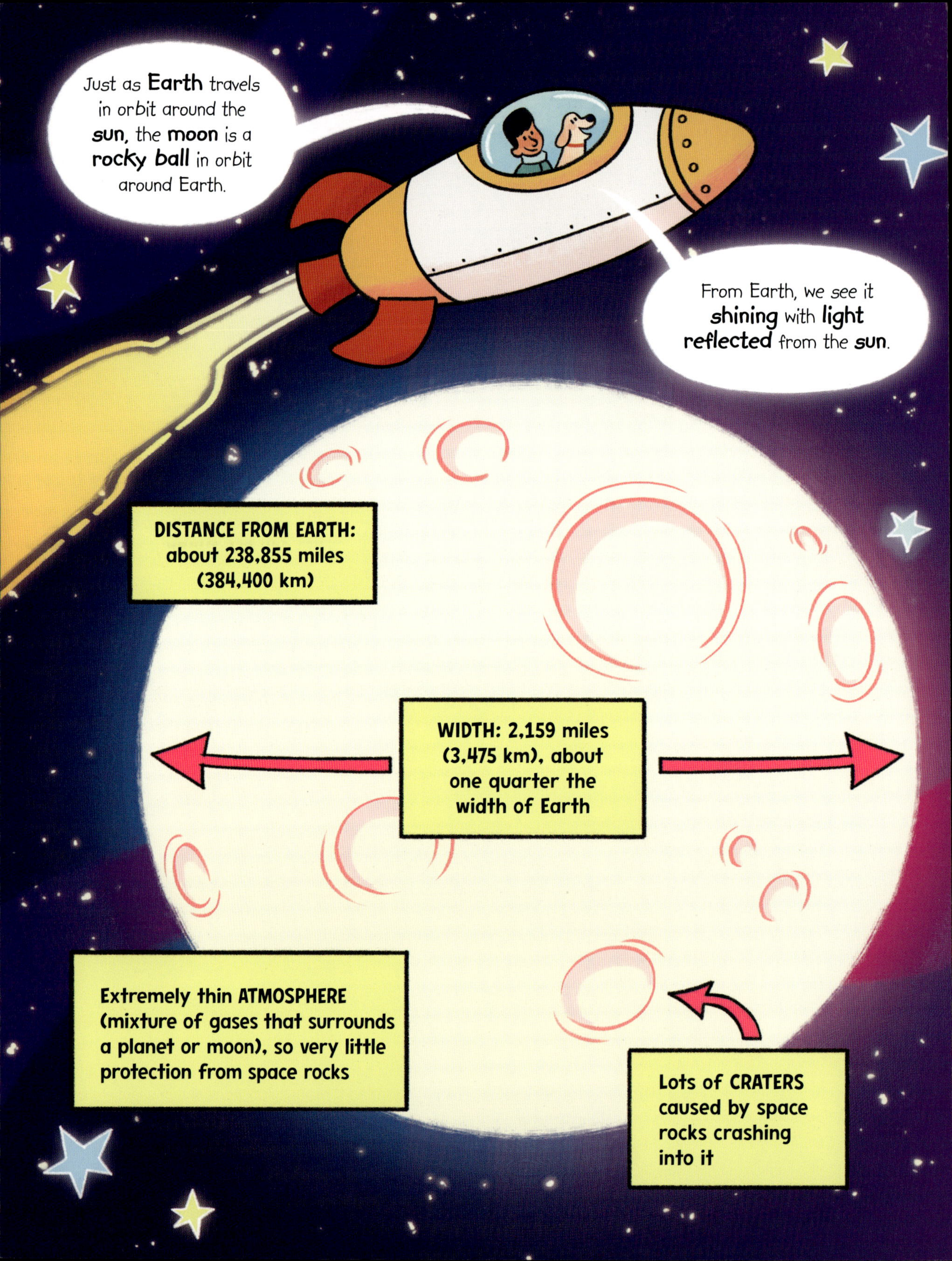
Just as **Earth** travels in orbit around the **sun**, the **moon** is a **rocky ball** in orbit around Earth.
From Earth, we see it **shining** with **light reflected** from the **sun**.
DISTANCE FROM EARTH: about 238,855 miles (384,400 km)
WIDTH: 2,159 miles (3,475 km), about one quarter the width of Earth
Extremely thin ATMOSPHERE (mixture of gases that surrounds a planet or moon), so very little protection from space rocks
Lots of CRATERS caused by space rocks crashing into it

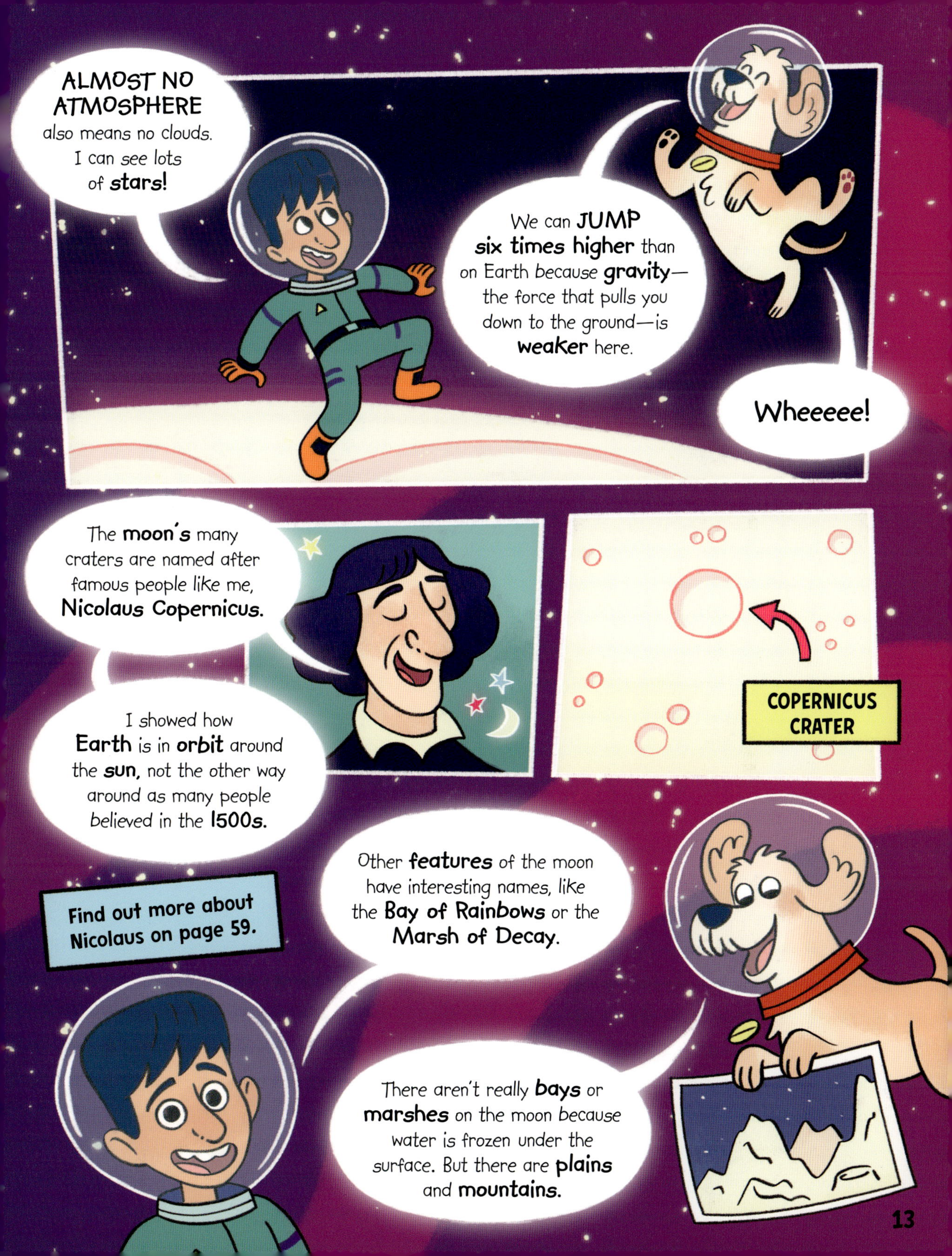
ALMOST NO ATMOSPHERE also means no clouds. I can see lots of stars!
We can JUMP six times higher than on Earth because gravity—the force that pulls you down to the ground—is weaker here.
Wheeeee!
The moon's many craters are named after famous people like me, Nicolaus Copernicus.
I showed how Earth is in orbit around the sun, not the other way around as many people believed in the 1500s.
COPERNICUS CRATER
Find out more about Nicolaus on page 59.
Other features of the moon have interesting names, like the Bay of Rainbows or the Marsh of Decay.
There aren't really bays or marshes on the moon because water is frozen under the surface. But there are plains and mountains.

When we look at the moon from Earth, it seems to change shape. The different shapes have names, and these are known as phases of the moon.

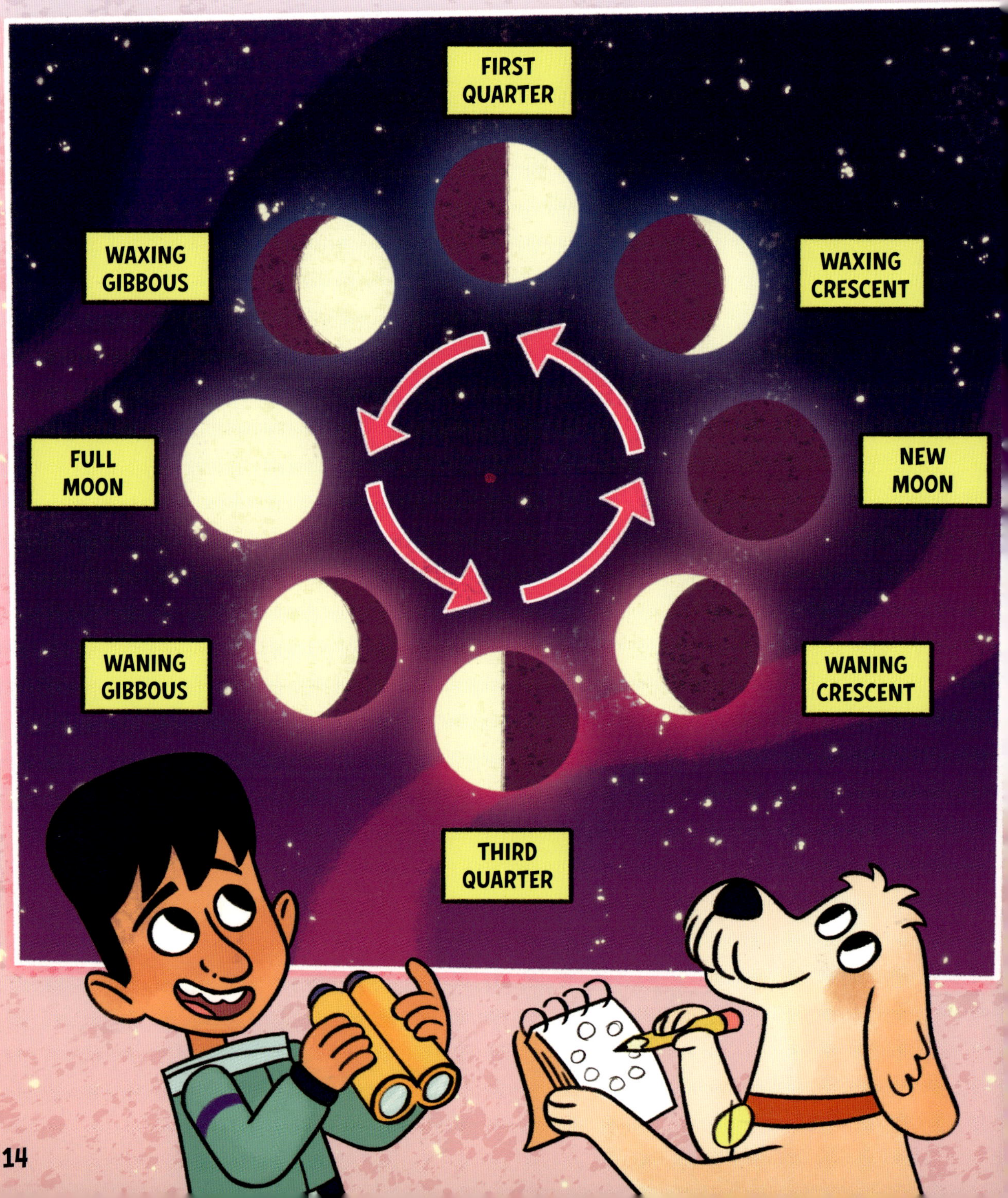
FIRST QUARTER
WAXING CRESCENT
NEW MOON
WANING CRESCENT
THIRD QUARTER
WANING GIBBOUS
FULL MOON
WAXING GIBBOUS

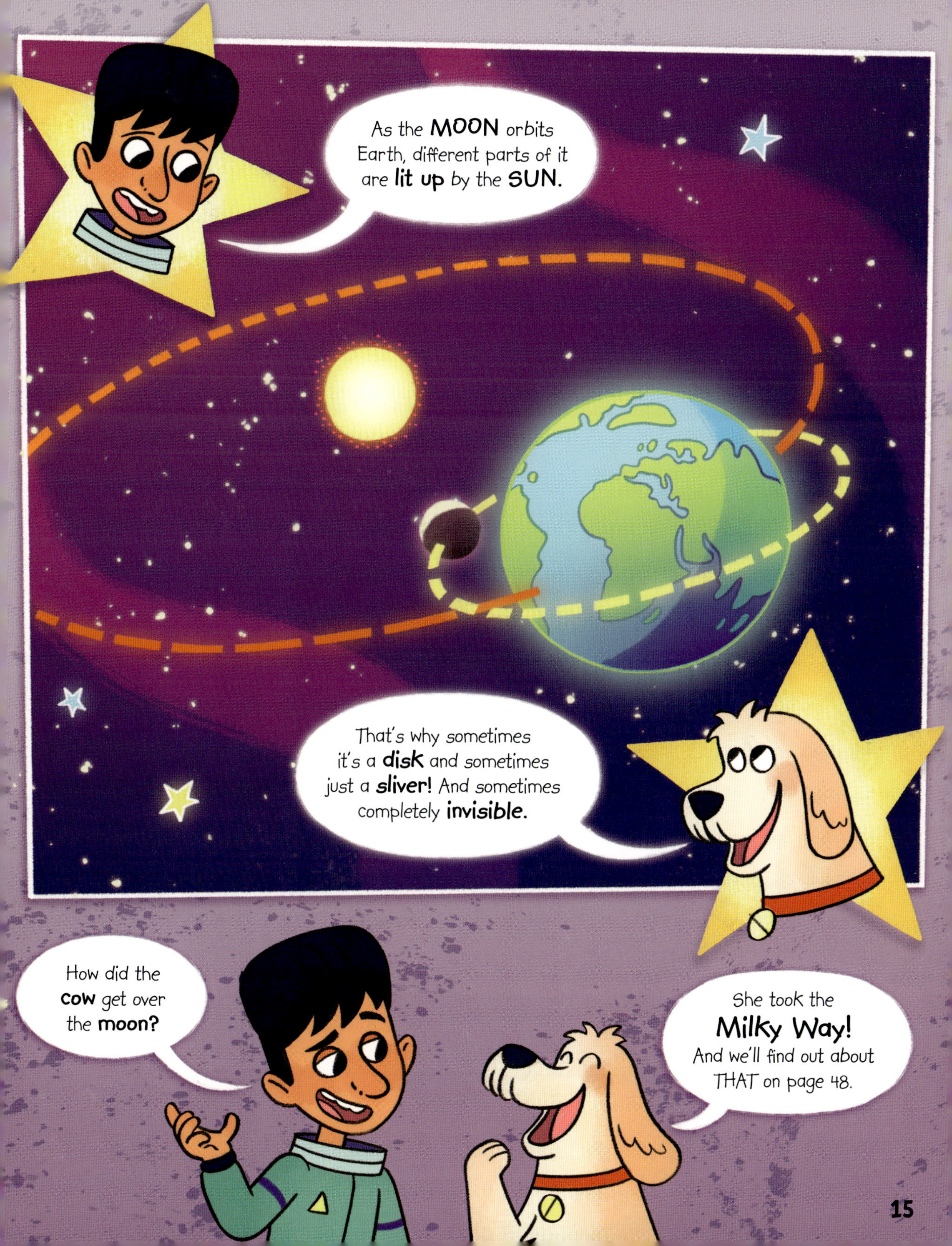
As the MOON orbits Earth, different parts of it are lit up by the SUN.
That's why sometimes it's a disk and sometimes just a sliver! And sometimes completely invisible.
How did the cow get over the moon?
She took the Milky Way! And we'll find out about THAT on page 48.

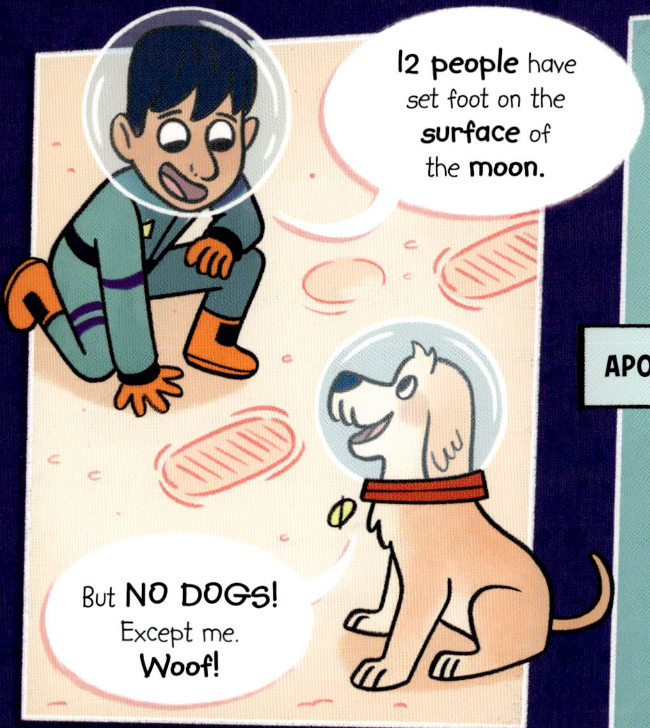
12 people have set foot on the surface of the moon.
But NO DOGS! Except me. Woof!

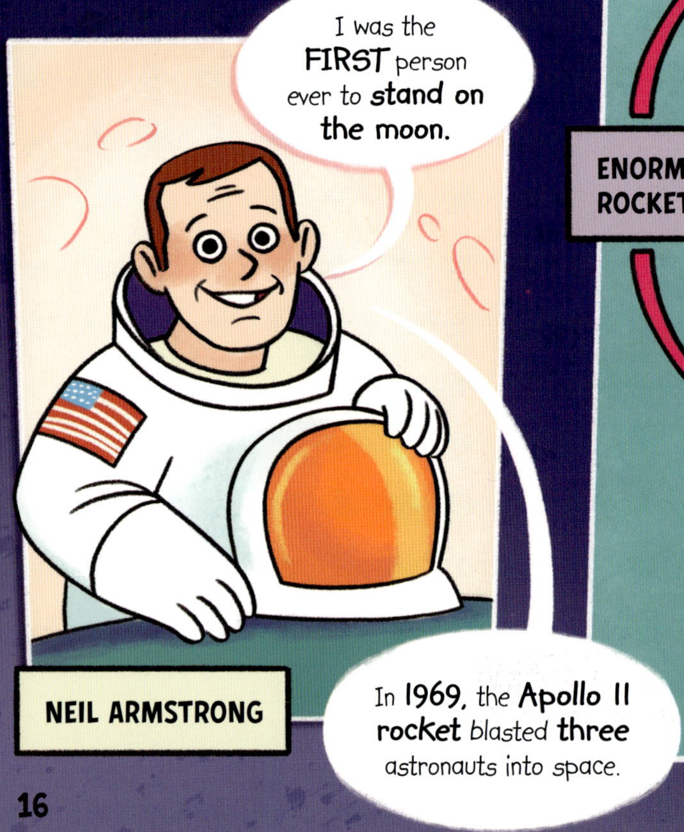
I was the FIRST person ever to stand on the moon.
NEIL ARMSTRONG
In 1969, the Apollo 11 rocket blasted three astronauts into space.

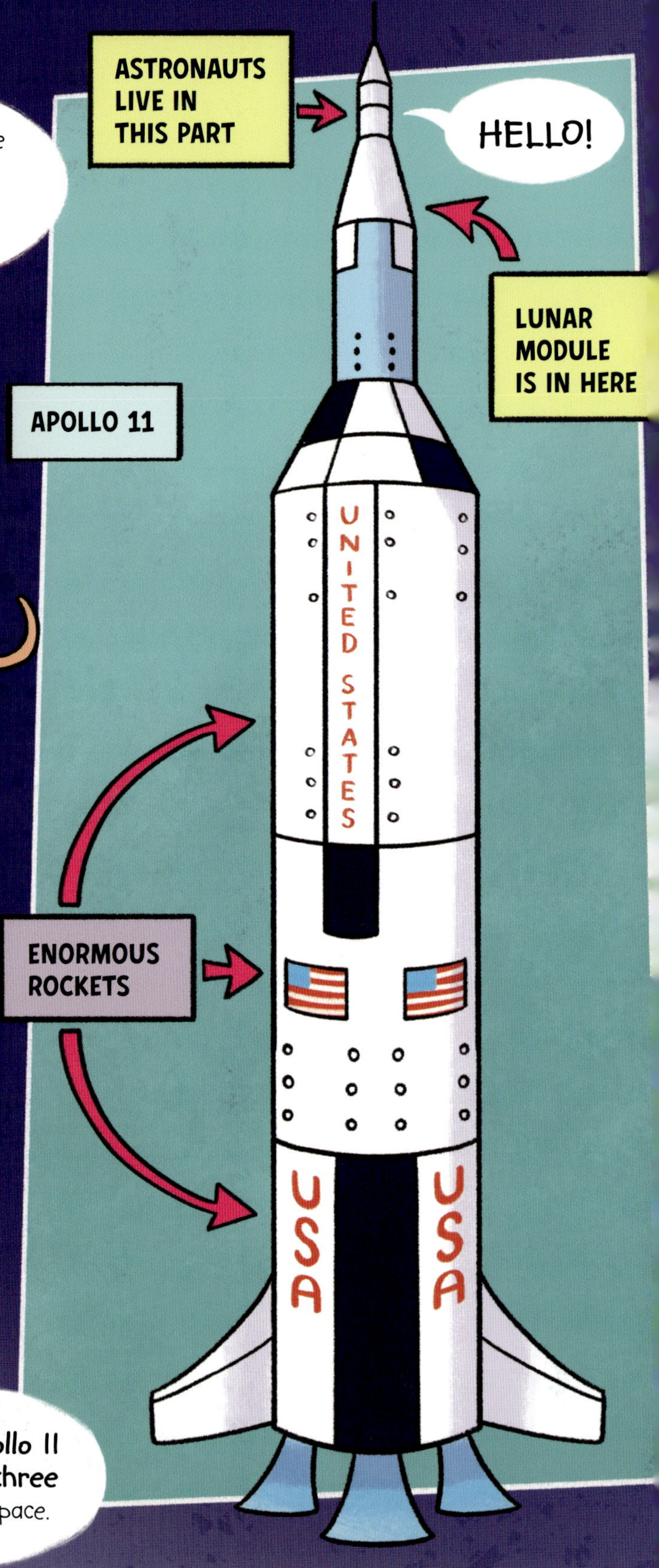
ASTRONAUTS LIVE IN THIS PART
HELLO!
LUNAR MODULE IS IN HERE
APOLLO 11
UNITED STATES
ENORMOUS ROCKETS
USA
USA

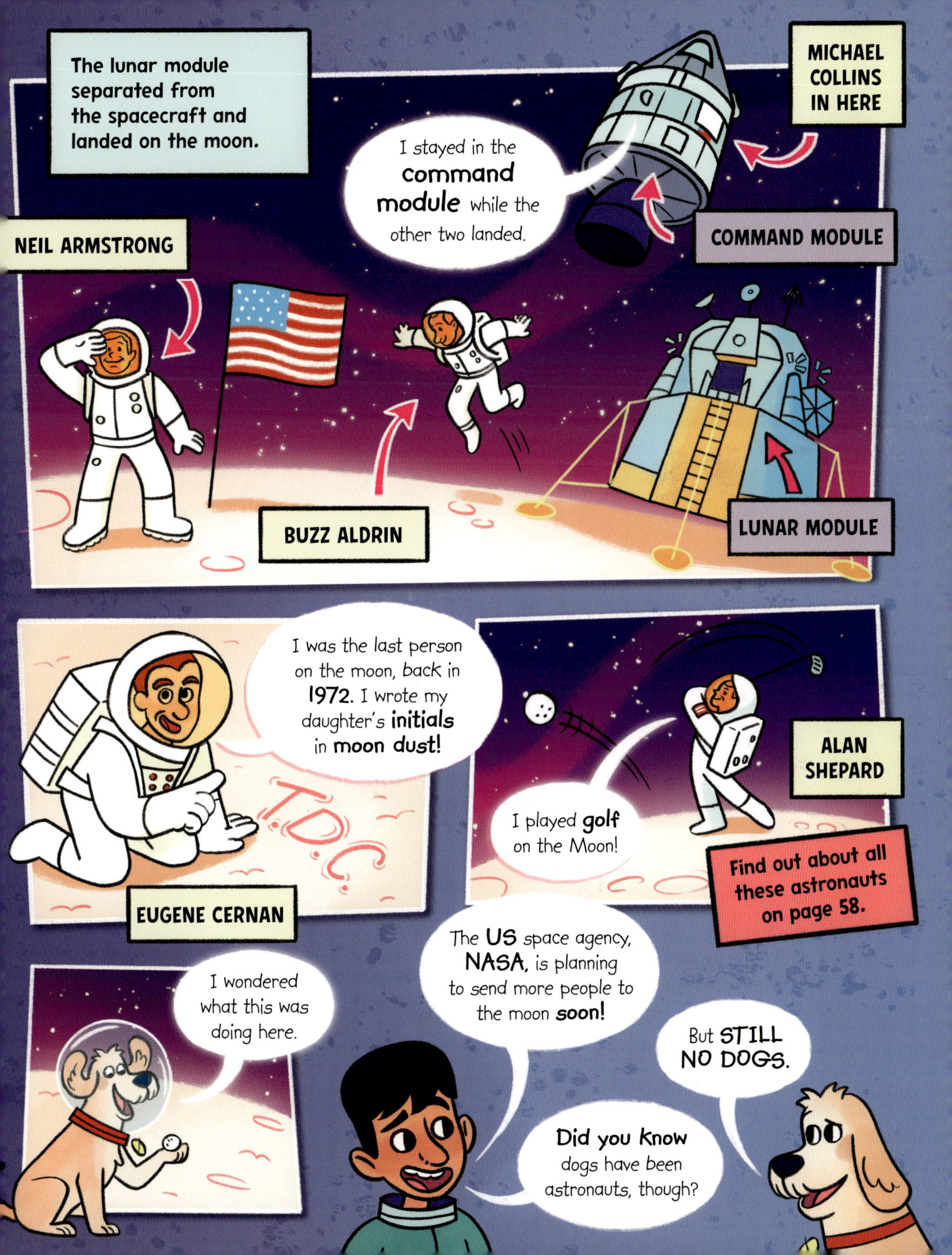
The lunar module separated from the spacecraft and landed on the moon.
I stayed in the command module while the other two landed.
MICHAEL COLLINS IN HERE
COMMAND MODULE
NEIL ARMSTRONG
BUZZ ALDRIN
LUNAR MODULE
I was the last person on the moon, back in 1972. I wrote my daughter's initials in moon dust!
T.D.C.
EUGENE CERNAN
I played golf on the Moon!
ALAN SHEPARD
Find out about all these astronauts on page 58.
I wondered what this was doing here.
The US space agency, NASA, is planning to send more people to the moon soon!
But STILL NO DOGS.
Did you know dogs have been astronauts, though?

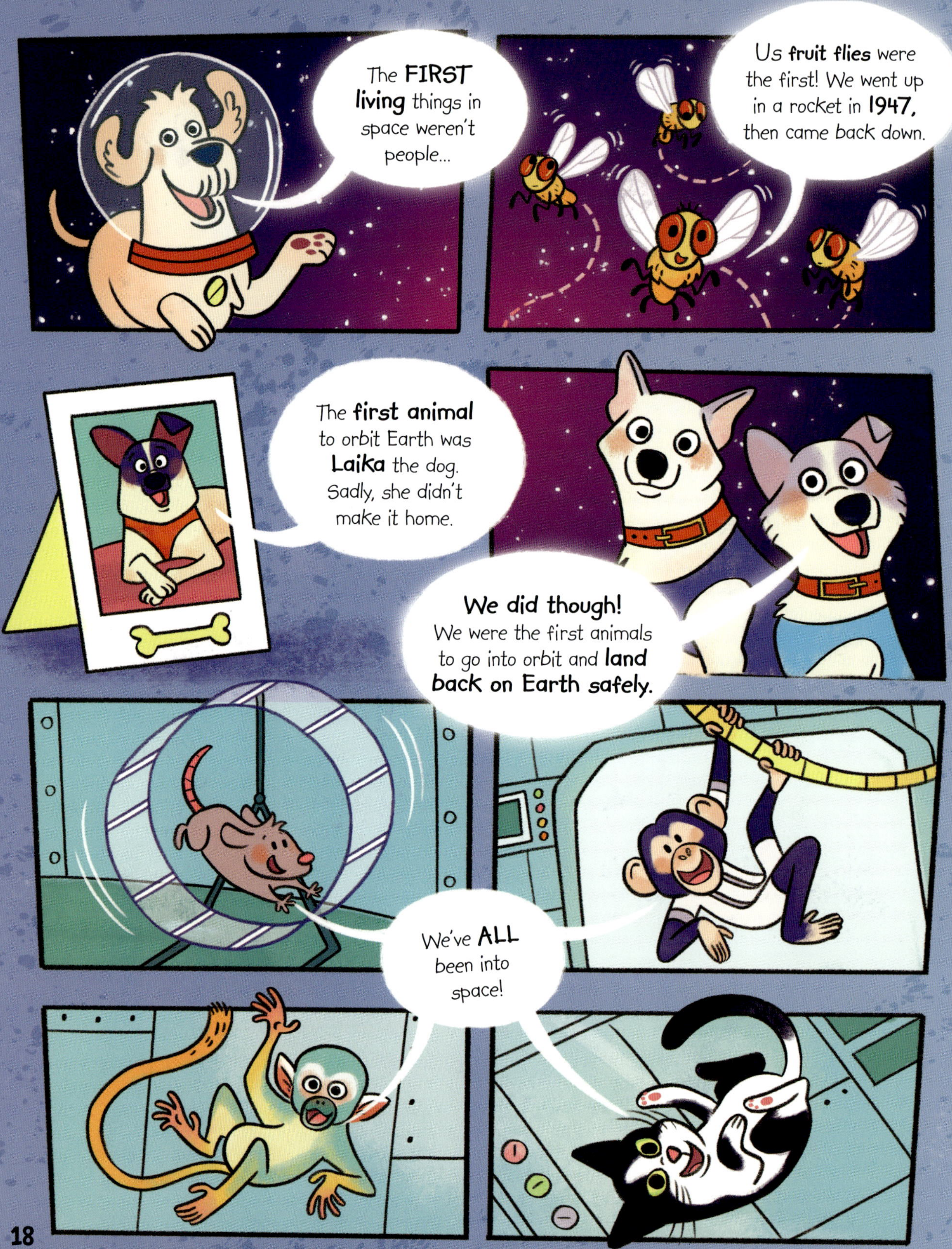

The **FIRST** **living** things in space weren't people...
Us **fruit flies** were the first! We went up in a rocket in **1947**, then came back down.
The **first animal** to orbit Earth was **Laika** the dog. Sadly, she didn't make it home.
**We did though!** We were the first animals to go into orbit and **land back on Earth safely.**
We've **ALL** been into space!

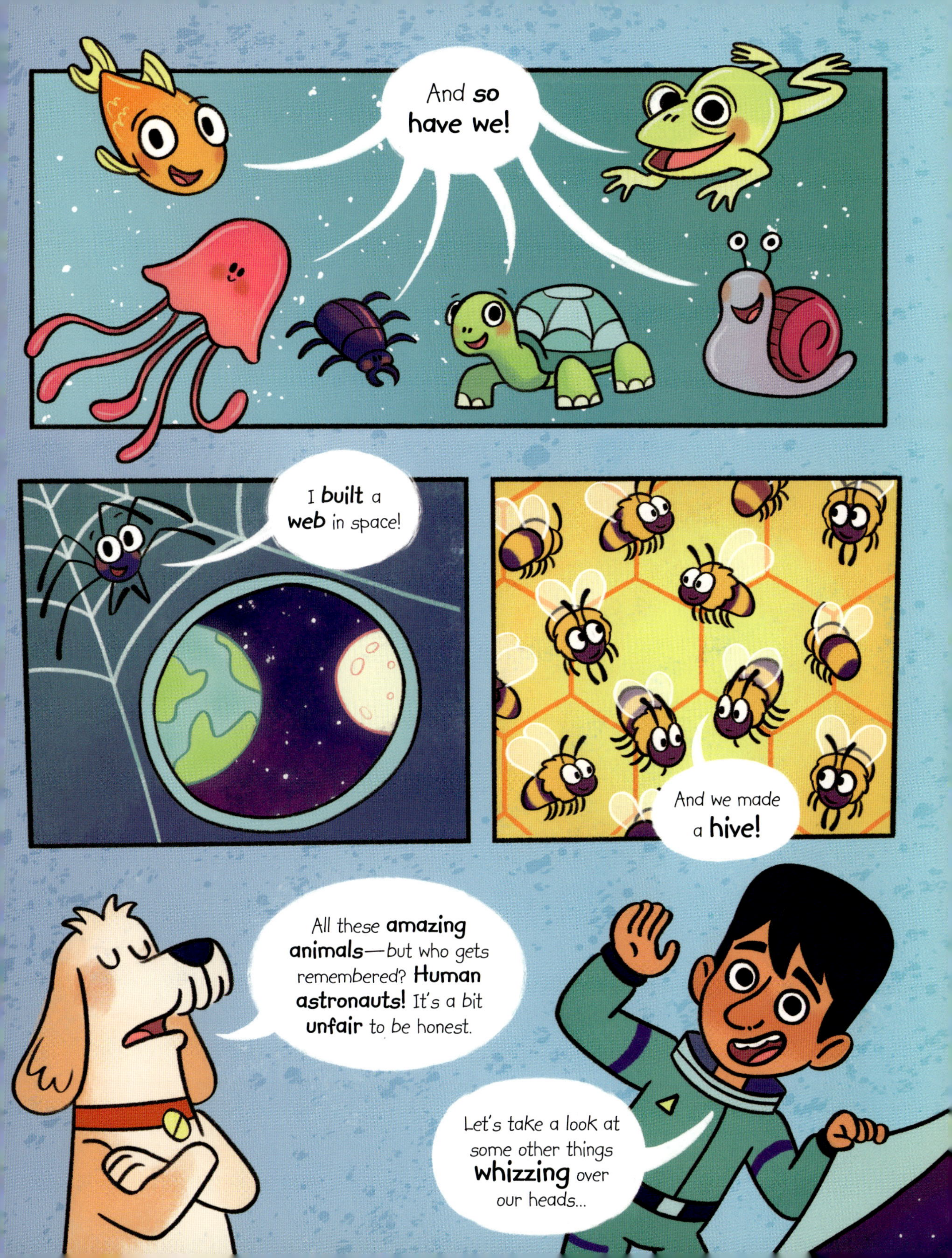
And so have we!
I built a web in space!
And we made a hive!
All these amazing animals—but who gets remembered? Human astronauts! It's a bit unfair to be honest.
Let's take a look at some other things whizzing over our heads...

The moon is Earth's only **NATURAL SATELLITE** (a satellite is something that orbits a planet or other object). But there are lots that we've put there...

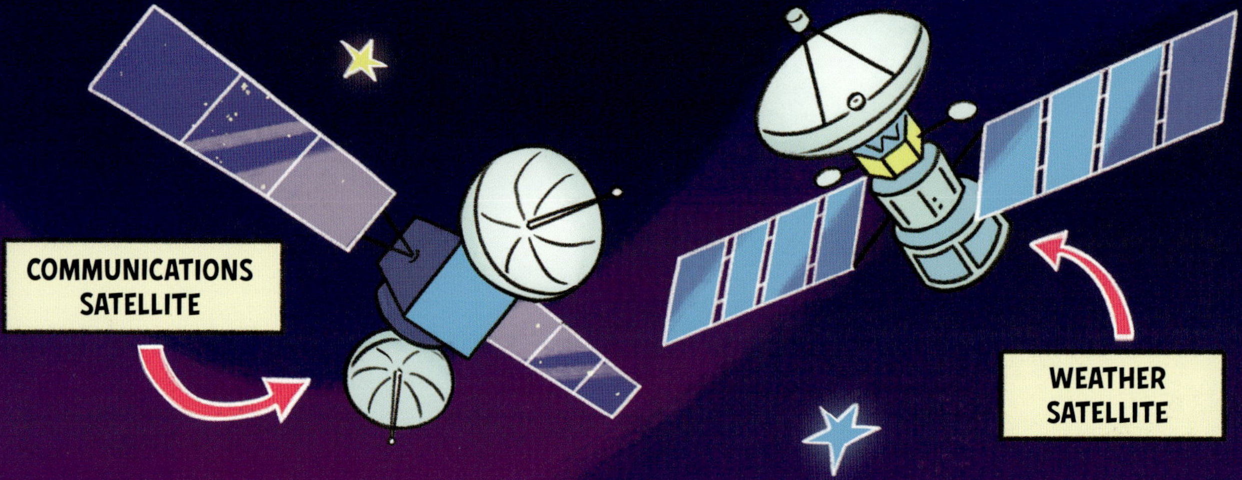
COMMUNICATIONS SATELLITE
WEATHER SATELLITE

Satellites can travel in various orbits, including **LOW EARTH, MIDDLE EARTH,** and **GEOSTATIONARY.**

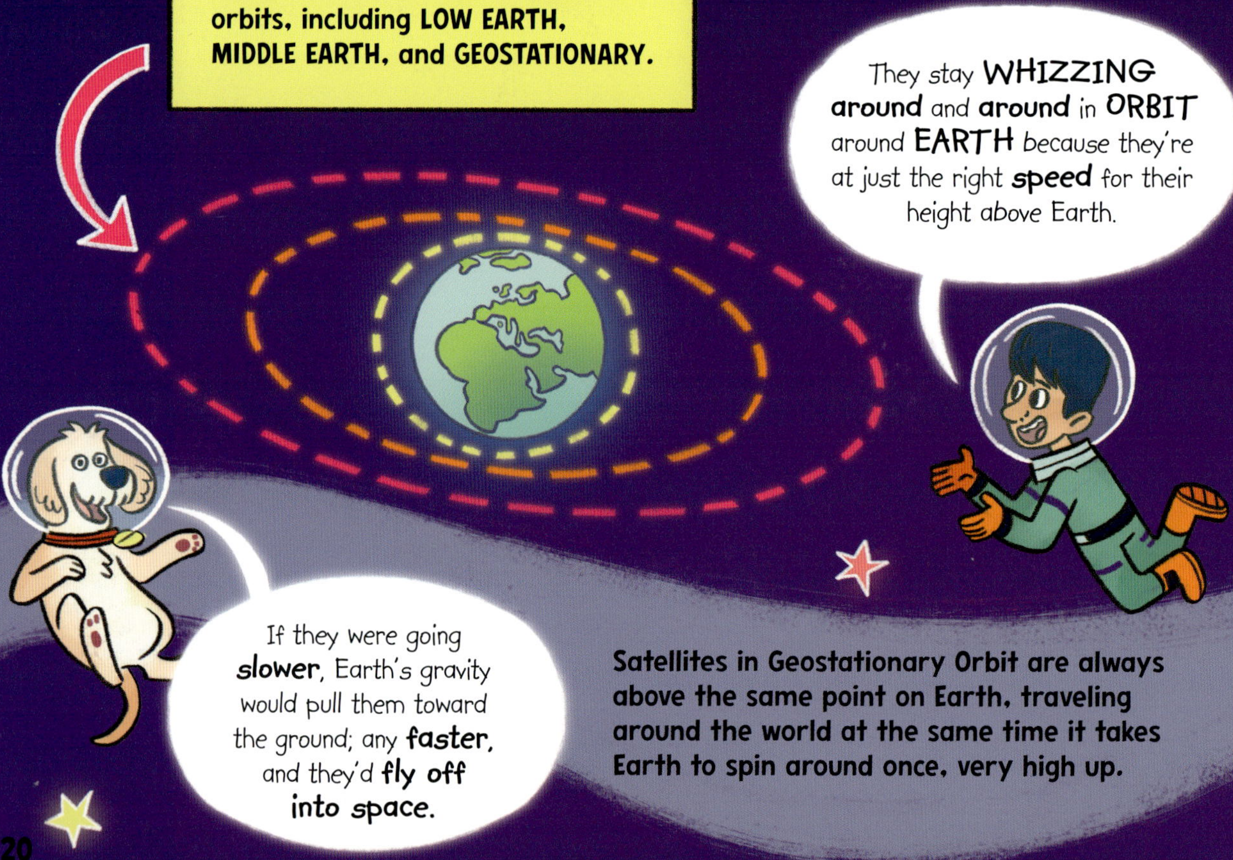
They stay WHIZZING around and around in ORBIT around EARTH because they're at just the right speed for their height above Earth.
If they were going slower, Earth's gravity would pull them toward the ground; any faster, and they'd fly off into space.

Satellites in Geostationary Orbit are always above the same point on Earth, traveling around the world at the same time it takes Earth to spin around once, very high up.

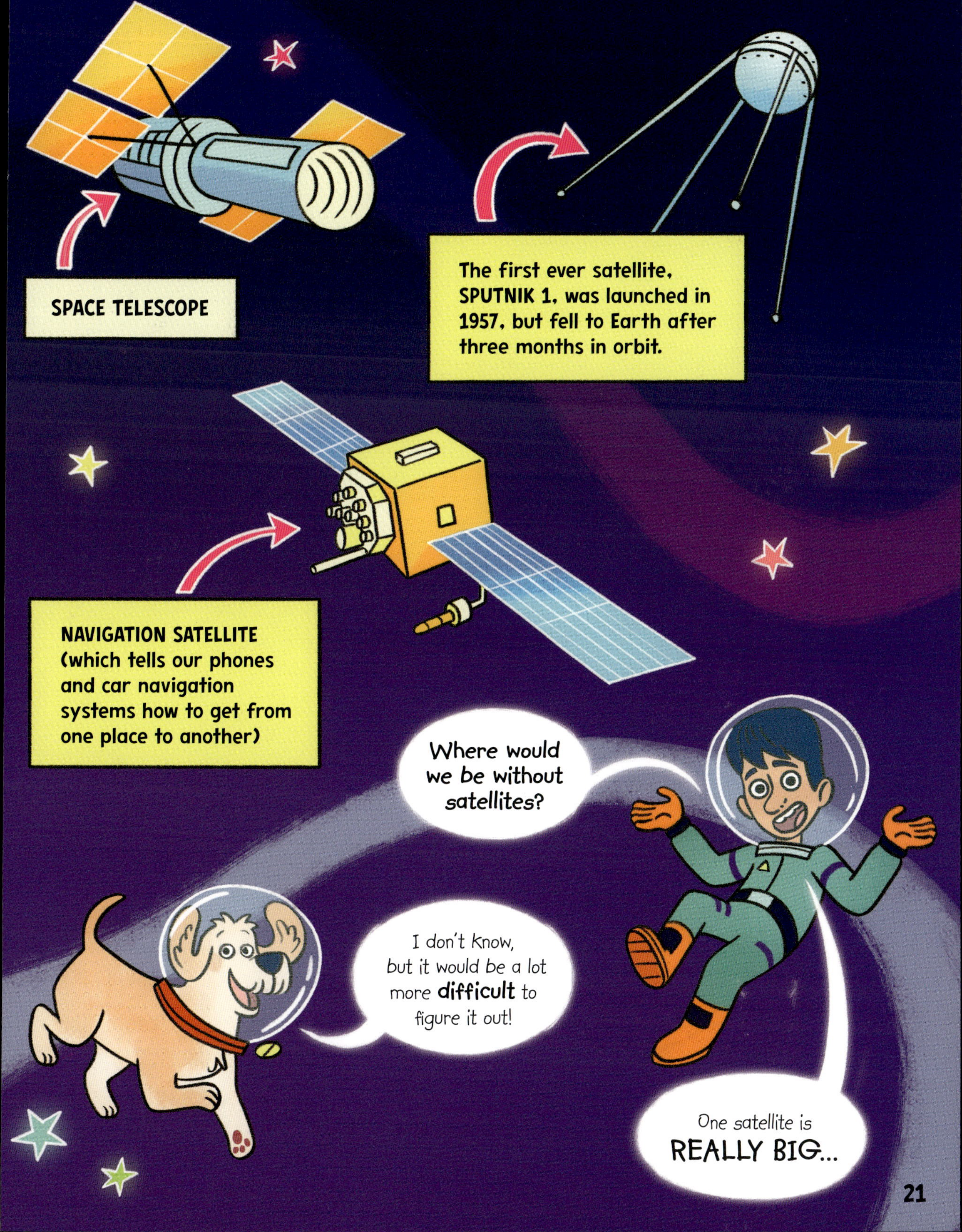

SPACE TELESCOPE
The first ever satellite, SPUTNIK 1, was launched in 1957, but fell to Earth after three months in orbit.
NAVIGATION SATELLITE (which tells our phones and car navigation systems how to get from one place to another)
Where would we be without satellites?
I don't know, but it would be a lot more **difficult** to figure it out!
One satellite is REALLY BIG...

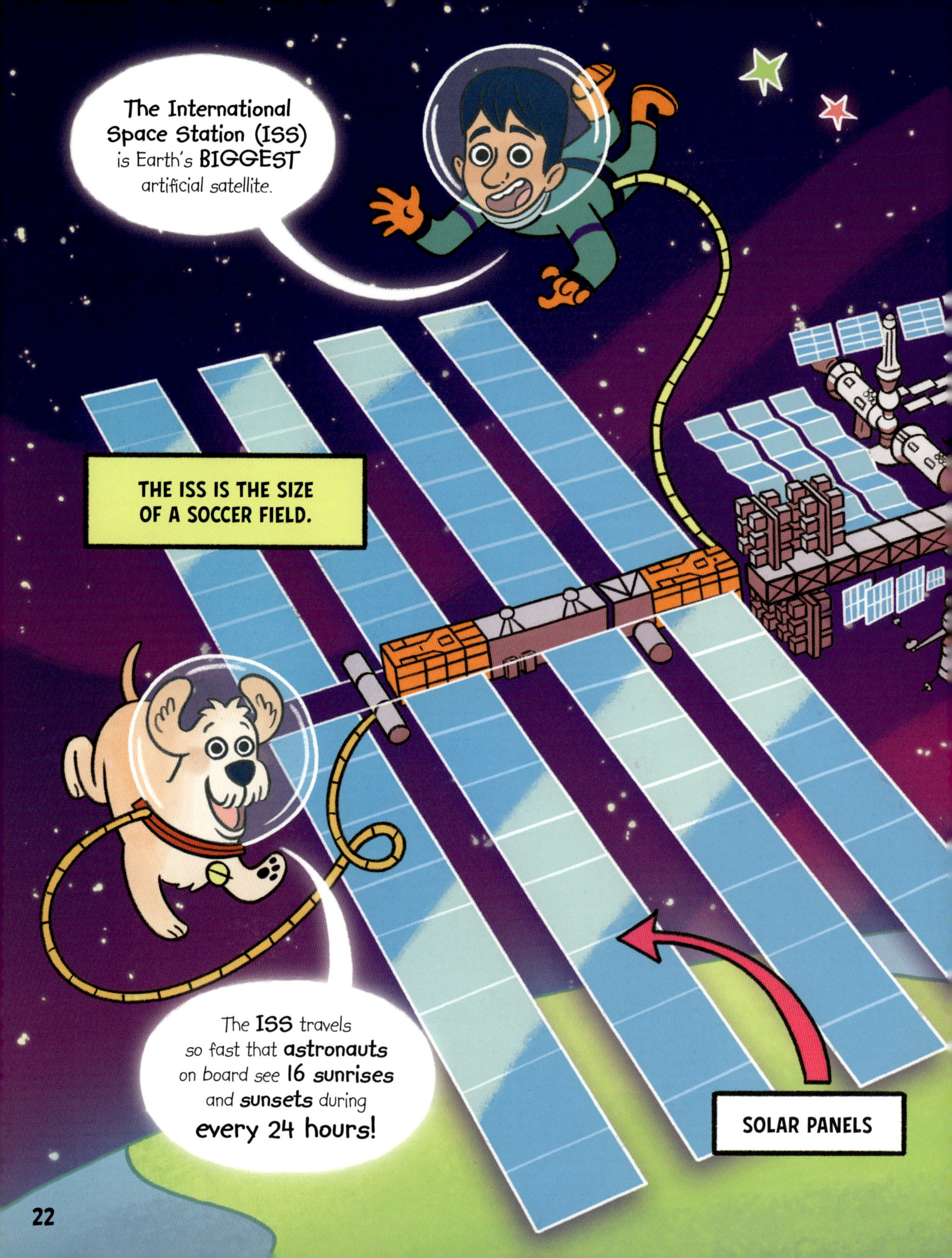

The International Space Station (ISS) is Earth's BIGGEST artificial satellite.
THE ISS IS THE SIZE OF A SOCCER FIELD.
The ISS travels so fast that astronauts on board see 16 sunrises and sunsets during every 24 hours!
SOLAR PANELS

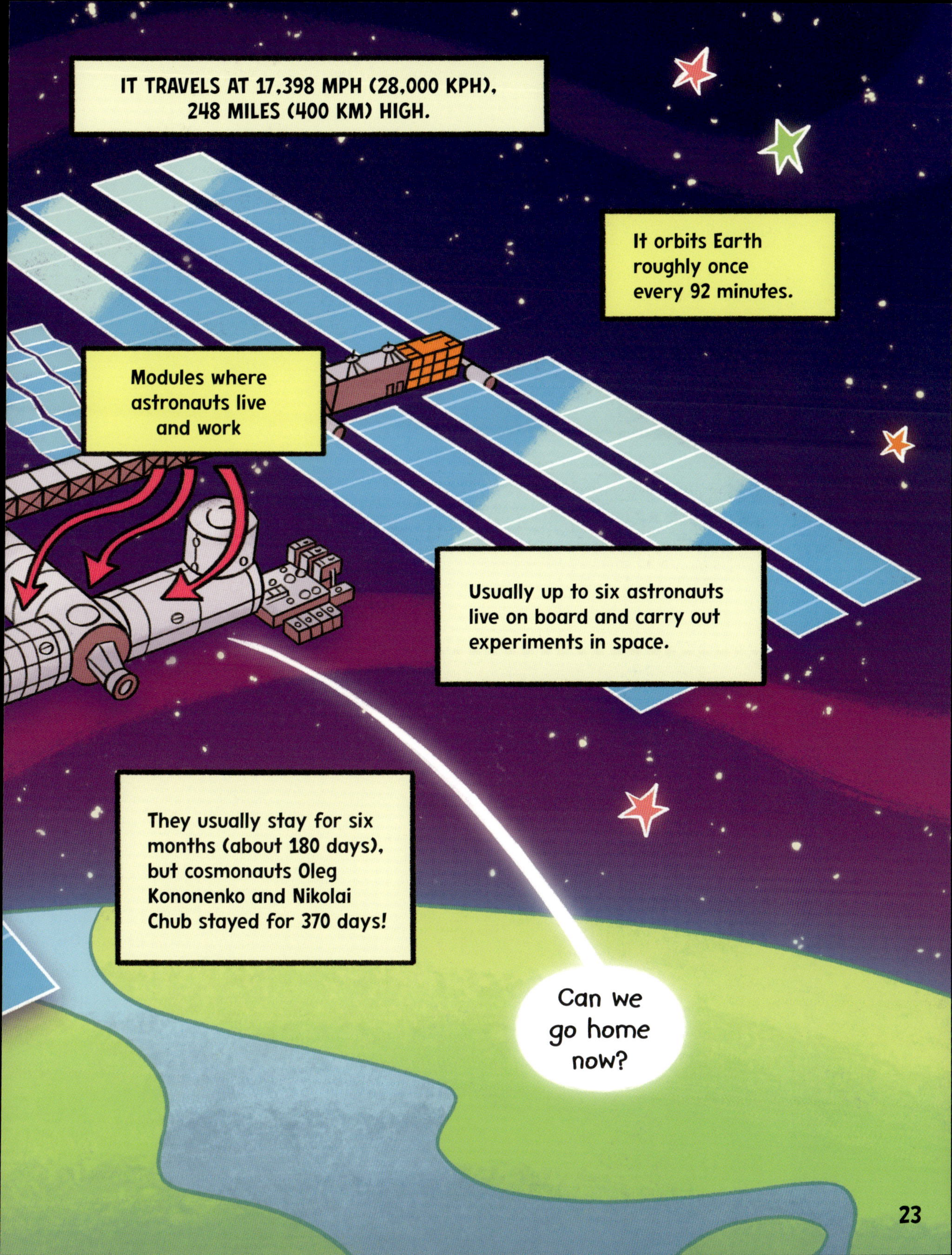
IT TRAVELS AT 17,398 MPH (28,000 KPH), 248 MILES (400 KM) HIGH.
It orbits Earth roughly once every 92 minutes.
Modules where astronauts live and work
Usually up to six astronauts live on board and carry out experiments in space.
They usually stay for six months (about 180 days), but cosmonauts Oleg Kononenko and Nikolai Chub stayed for 370 days!
Can we go home now?

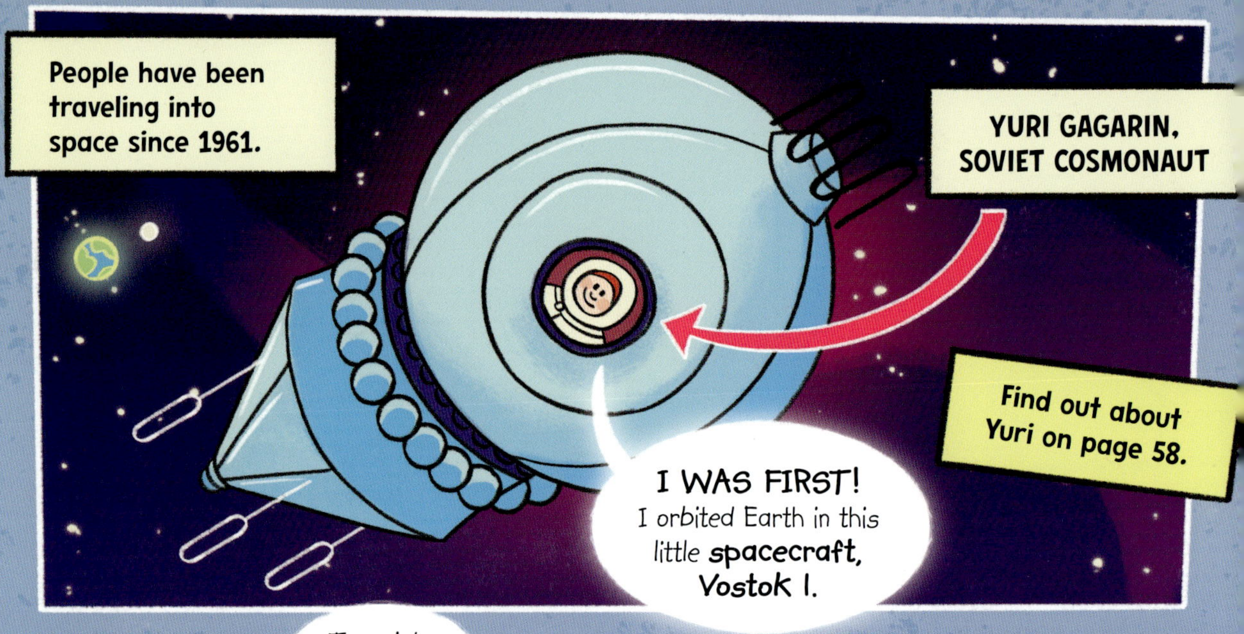
People have been traveling into space since 1961.
YURI GAGARIN, SOVIET COSMONAUT
Find out about Yuri on page 58.
I WAS FIRST! I orbited Earth in this little spacecraft, Vostok I.

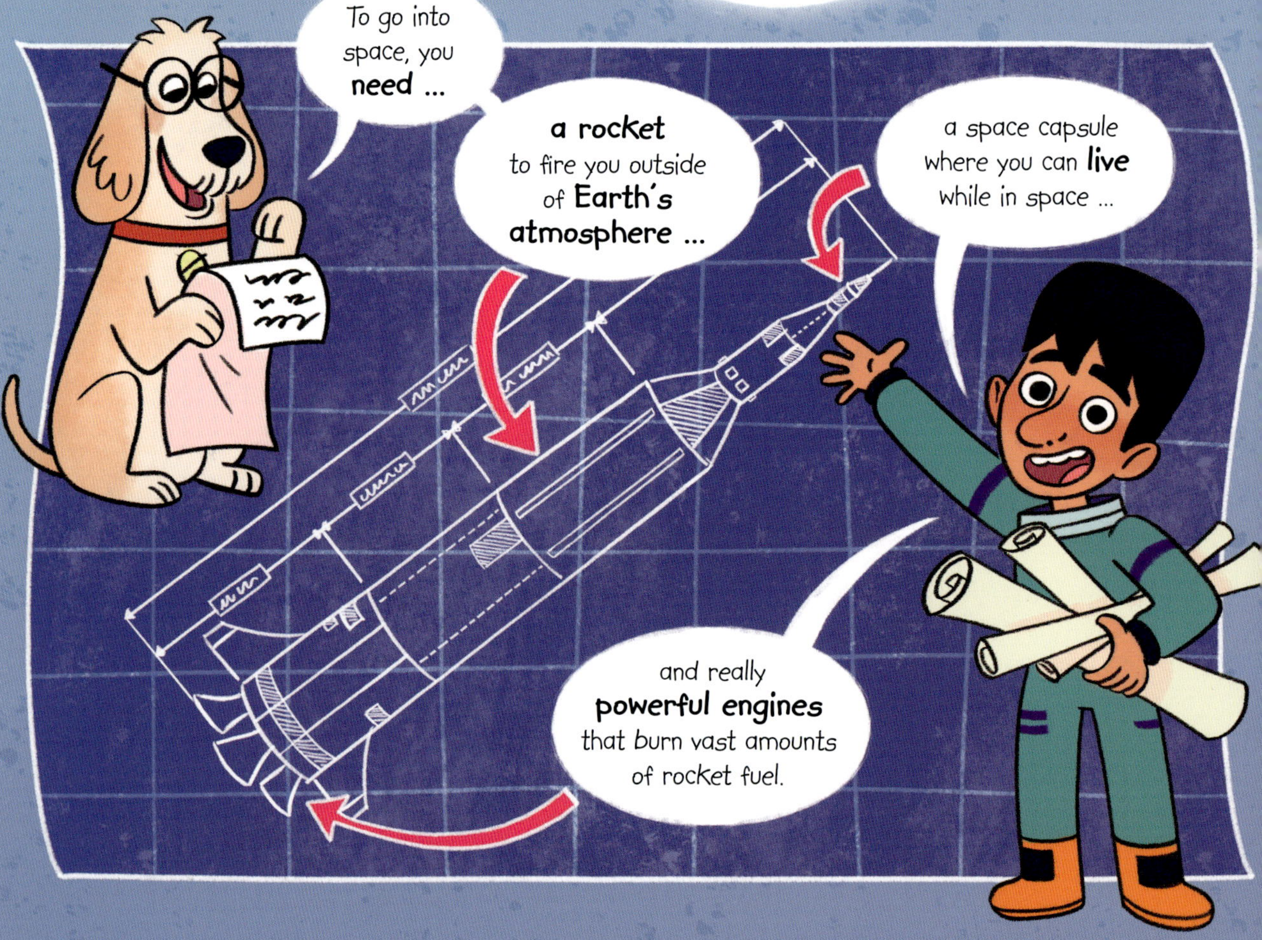
To go into space, you need ...
a rocket to fire you outside of Earth's atmosphere ...
a space capsule where you can live while in space ...
and really powerful engines that burn vast amounts of rocket fuel.

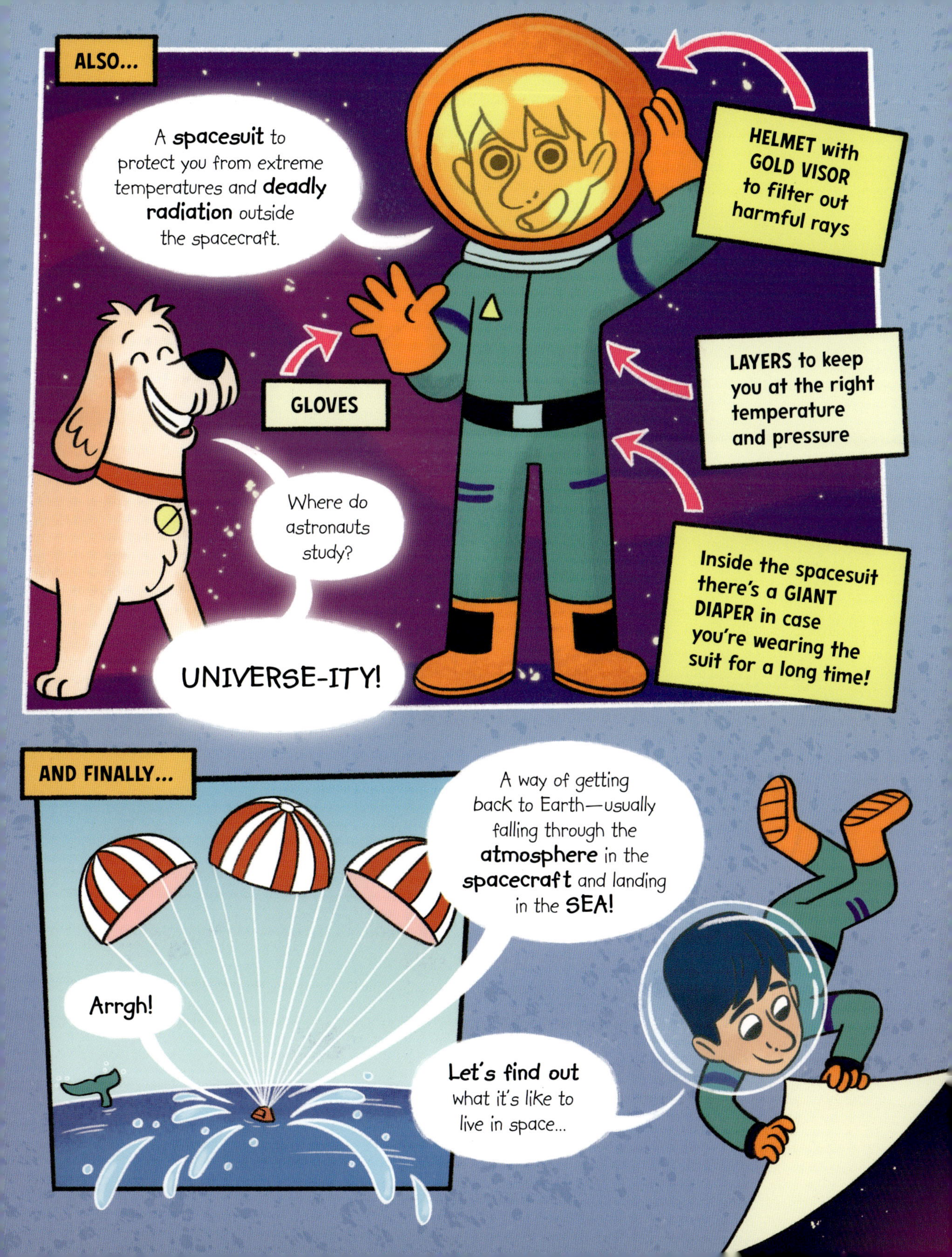
ALSO...
A spacesuit to protect you from extreme temperatures and deadly radiation outside the spacecraft.
HELMET with GOLD VISOR to filter out harmful rays
GLOVES
LAYERS to keep you at the right temperature and pressure
Where do astronauts study?
UNIVERSE-ITY!
Inside the spacesuit there's a GIANT DIAPER in case you're wearing the suit for a long time!
AND FINALLY...
A way of getting back to Earth—usually falling through the atmosphere in the spacecraft and landing in the SEA!
Arrgh!
Let's find out what it's like to live in space...

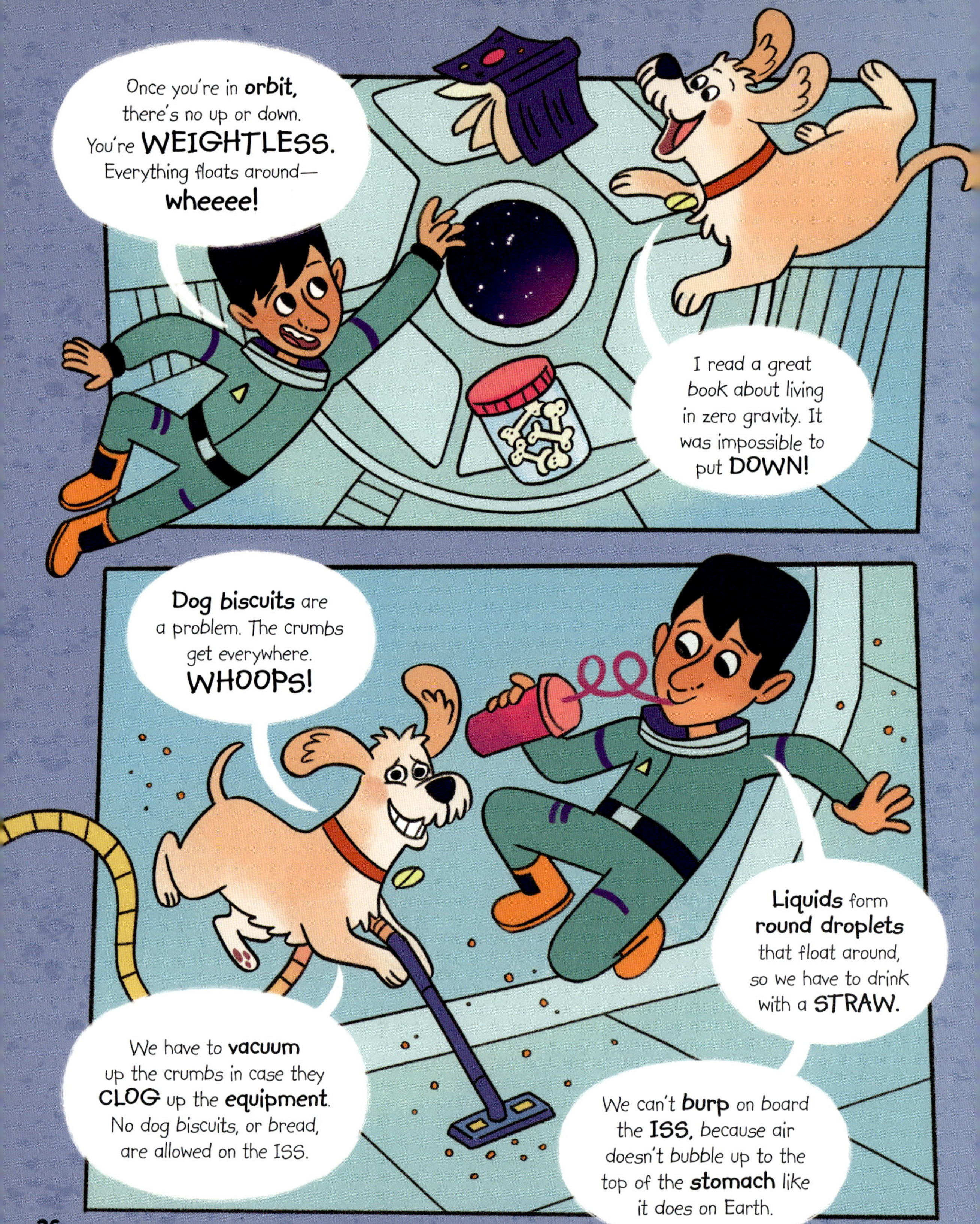

Once you're in orbit, there's no up or down. You're WEIGHTLESS. Everything floats around—wheeee!
I read a great book about living in zero gravity. It was impossible to put DOWN!
Dog biscuits are a problem. The crumbs get everywhere. WHOOPS!
Liquids form round droplets that float around, so we have to drink with a STRAW.
We have to vacuum up the crumbs in case they CLOG up the equipment. No dog biscuits, or bread, are allowed on the ISS.
We can't burp on board the ISS, because air doesn't bubble up to the top of the stomach like it does on Earth.

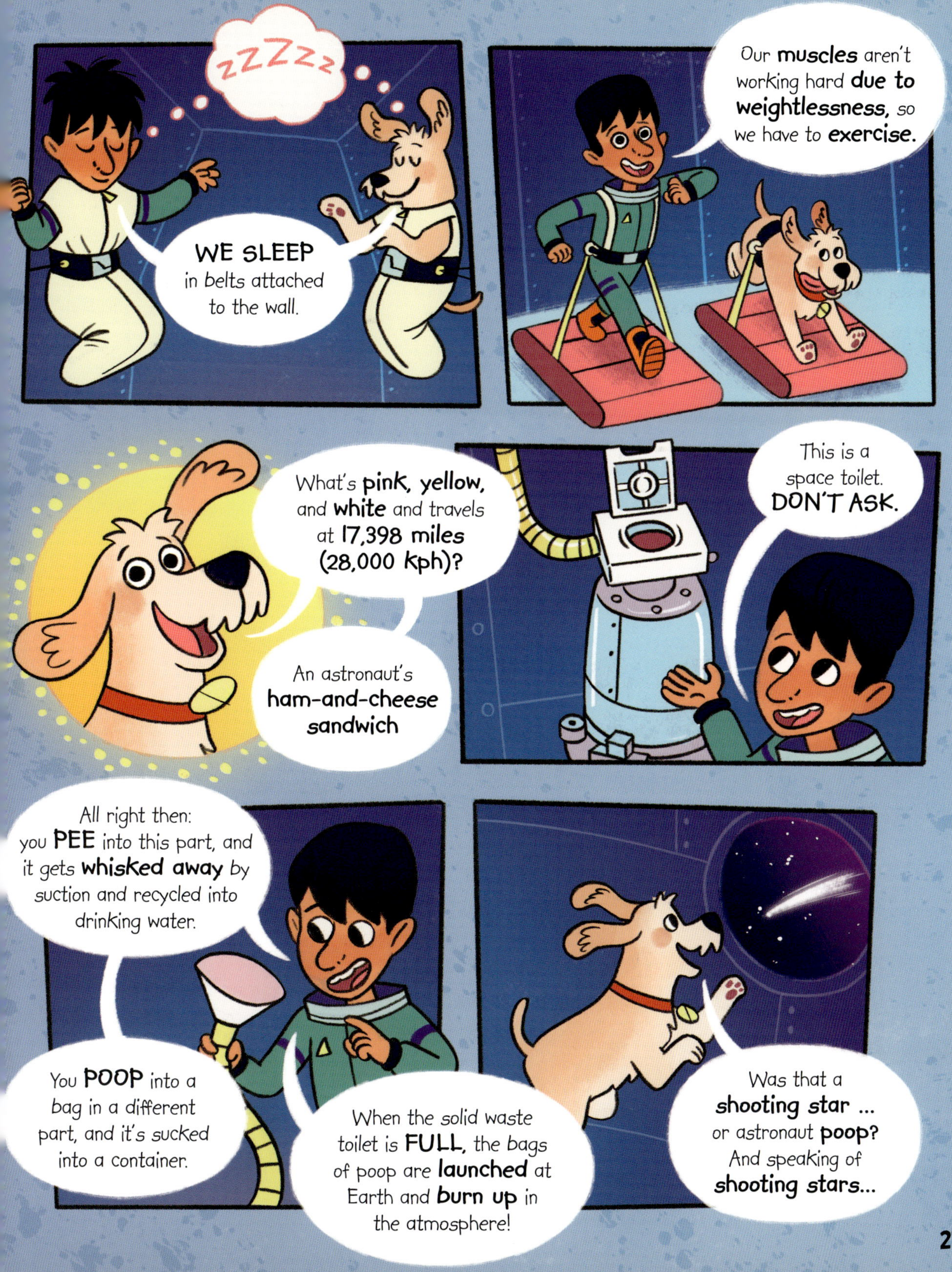
zZZZzz
WE SLEEP in belts attached to the wall.
Our muscles aren't working hard due to weightlessness, so we have to exercise.
What's pink, yellow, and white and travels at 17,398 miles (28,000 kph)?
An astronaut's ham-and-cheese sandwich
This is a space toilet. DON'T ASK.
All right then: you PEE into this part, and it gets whisked away by suction and recycled into drinking water.
You POOP into a bag in a different part, and it's sucked into a container.
When the solid waste toilet is FULL, the bags of poop are launched at Earth and burn up in the atmosphere!
Was that a shooting star ... or astronaut poop? And speaking of shooting stars...

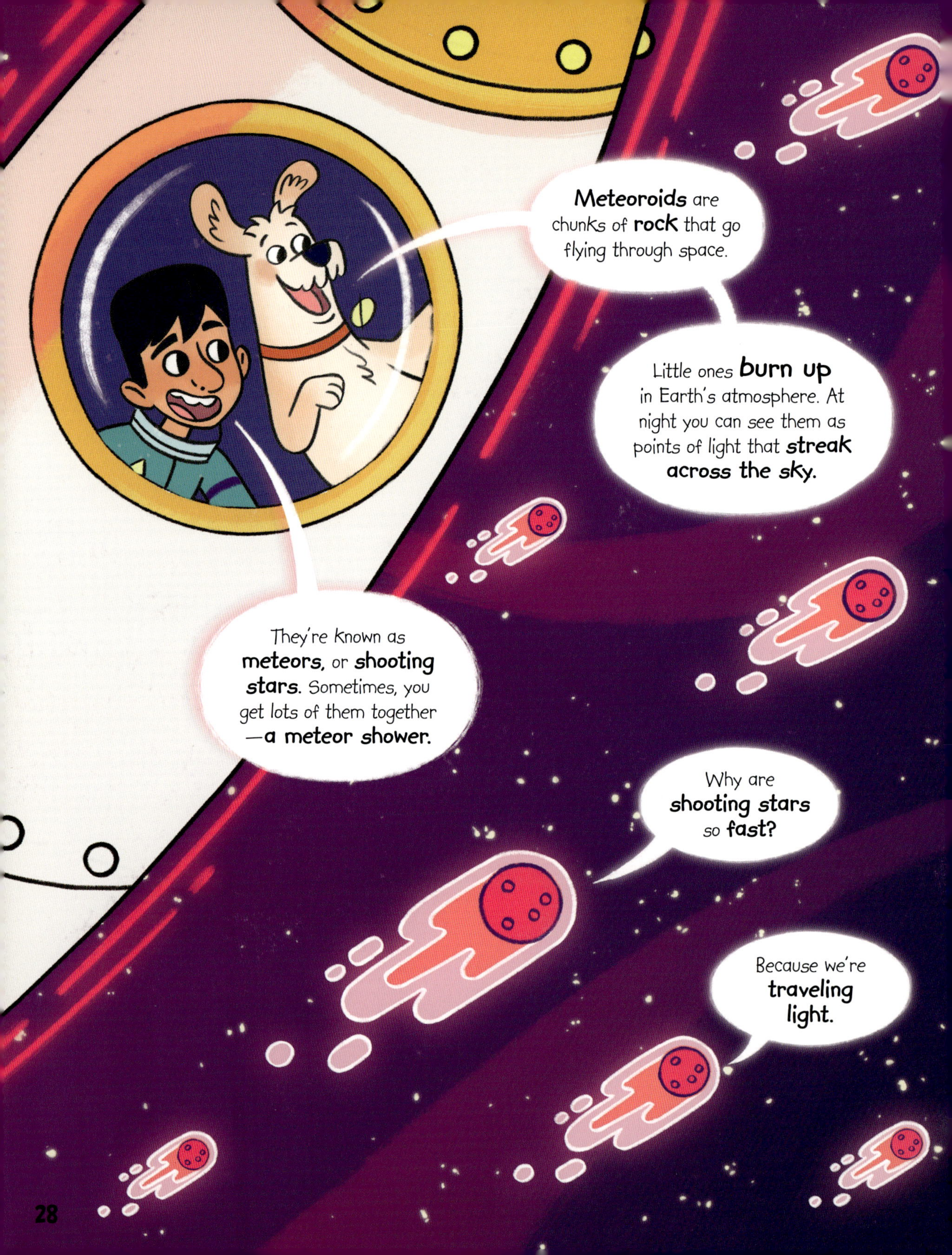
Meteoroids are chunks of rock that go flying through space.
Little ones burn up in Earth's atmosphere. At night you can see them as points of light that streak across the sky.
They're known as meteors, or shooting stars. Sometimes, you get lots of them together —a meteor shower.
Why are shooting stars so fast?
Because we're traveling light.

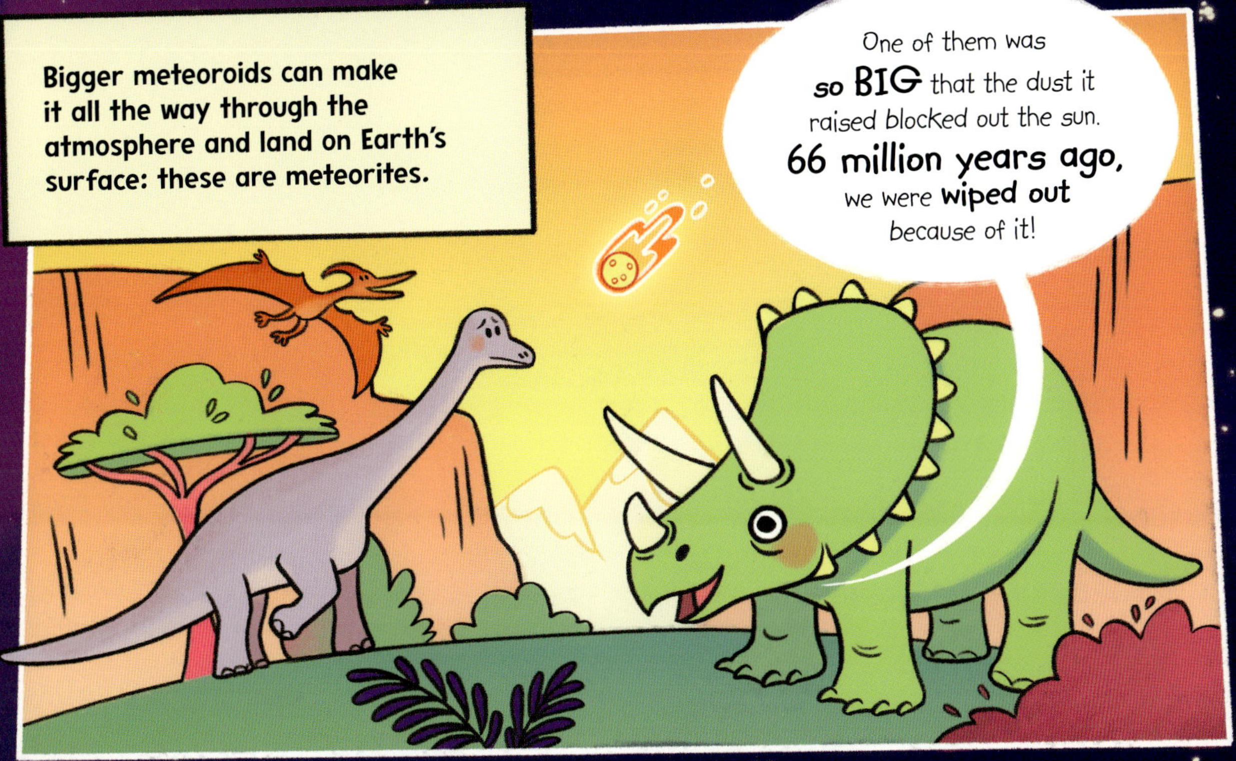
Bigger meteoroids can make it all the way through the atmosphere and land on Earth's surface: these are meteorites.
One of them was so BIG that the dust it raised blocked out the sun. 66 million years ago, we were wiped out because of it!

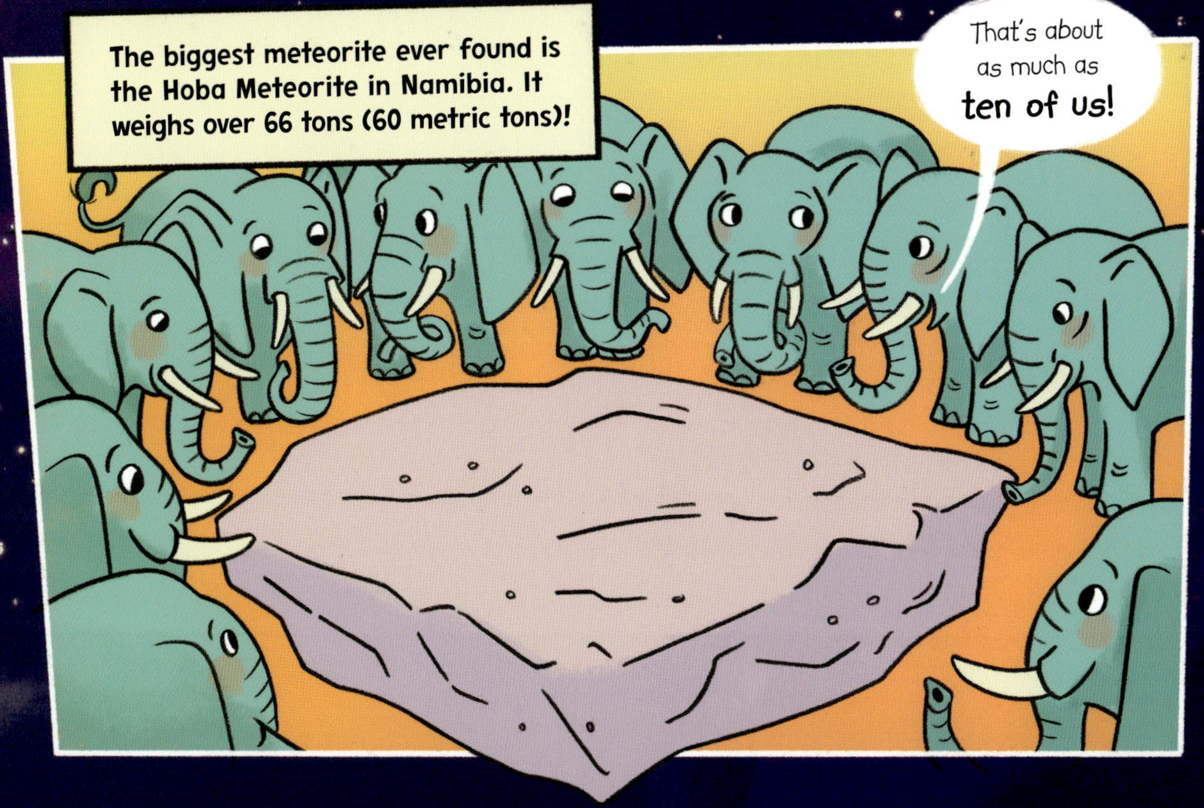
The biggest meteorite ever found is the Hoba Meteorite in Namibia. It weighs over 66 tons (60 metric tons)!
That's about as much as ten of us!

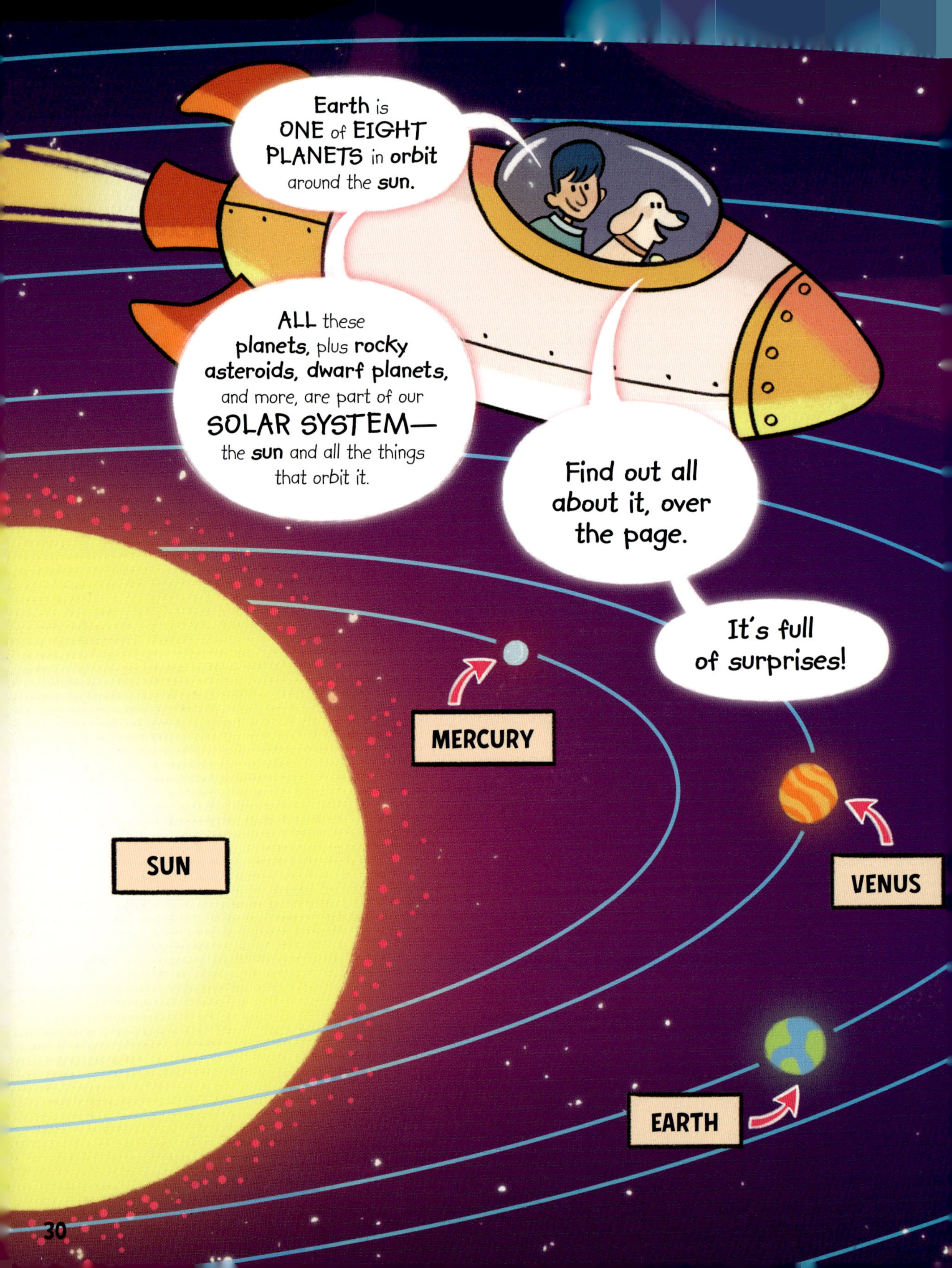
Earth is ONE of EIGHT PLANETS in orbit around the sun.
ALL these planets, plus rocky asteroids, dwarf planets, and more, are part of our SOLAR SYSTEM— the sun and all the things that orbit it.
Find out all about it, over the page.
It's full of surprises!
MERCURY
SUN
VENUS
EARTH

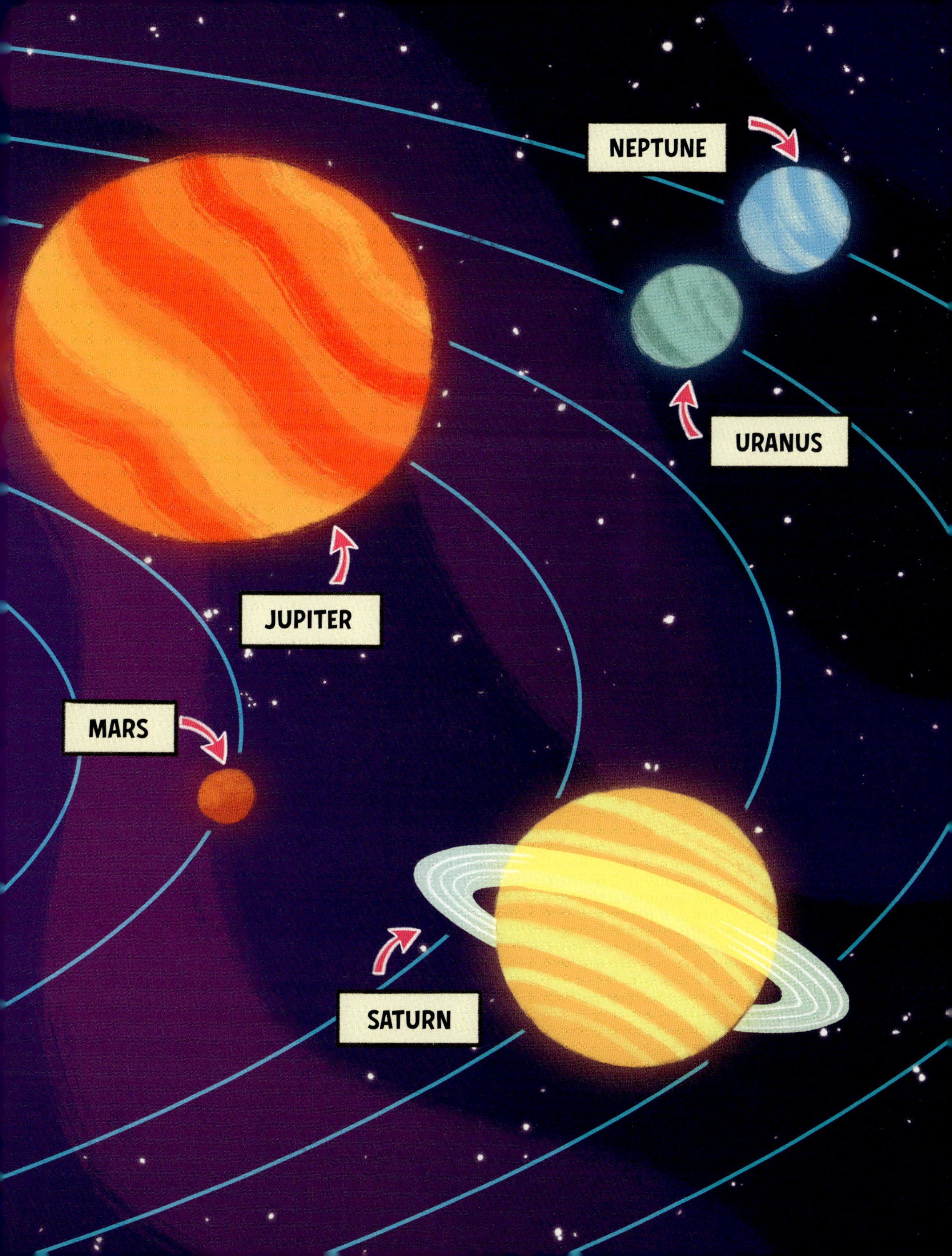
NEPTUNE
URANUS
JUPITER
MARS
SATURN

# MERCURY

## NAMED AFTER THE ANCIENT ROMAN MESSENGER GOD

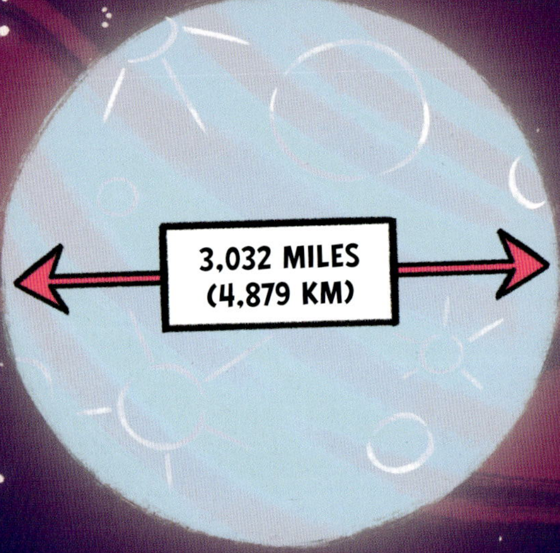
3,032 MILES
(4,879 KM)

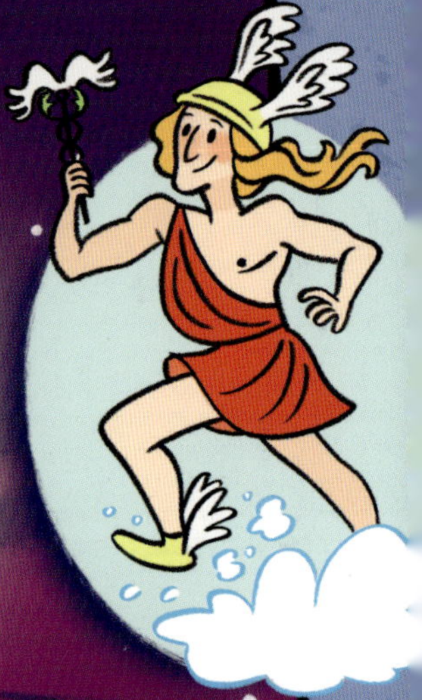

Closest planet to the sun and smallest planet in the solar system

The time it takes to spin around once (one Mercury day): 59 DAYS

The time it takes to orbit the sun (one Mercury year): 88 DAYS

Moons: 0

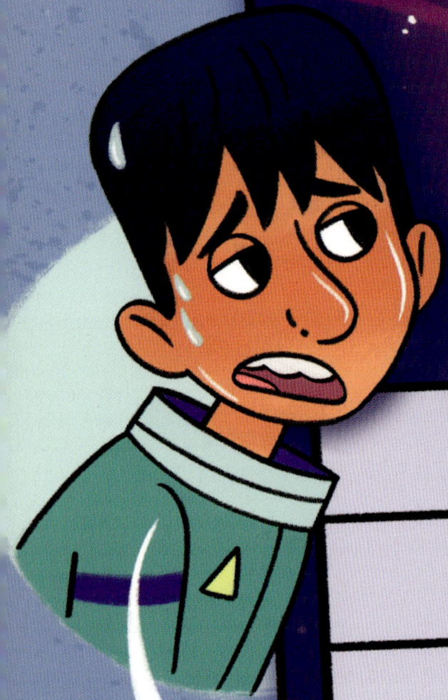
There's a **BIG** difference between **day** and **night** on **Mercury** ... **Daytime** temperatures can be **806°F (430°C)**, hot enough to **melt lead** ...

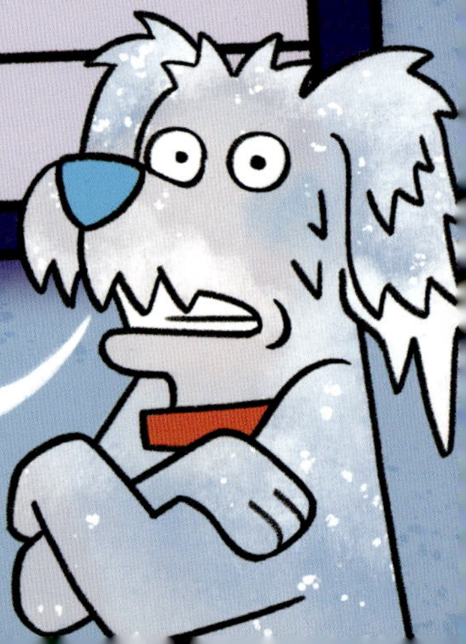
And at night, it's **MINUS 356°F (180°C)!!! Brrrrr.**

All the major planets in our solar system, except for Earth, are named after **ancient Roman gods and goddesses.**

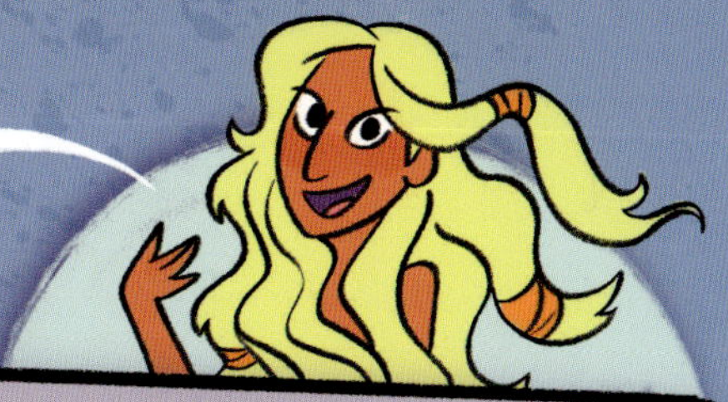

# VENUS

## NAMED AFTER THE ANCIENT ROMAN GODDESS OF LOVE

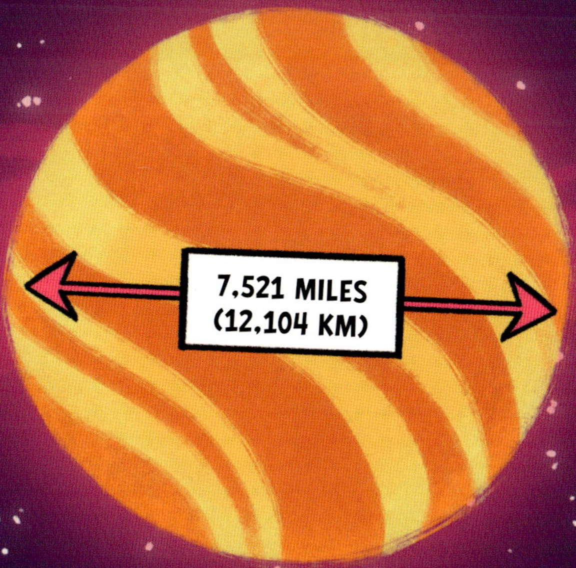
7,521 MILES
(12,104 KM)

| |
|---|
| Covered by clouds of sulfuric acid (which can dissolve metal) |
| The time it takes to spin around once (one Venus day): 243 DAYS |
| The time it takes to orbit the sun (one Venus year): 245 DAYS |
| Moons: 0 |

**A day** is almost the same as a year on **Venus.**

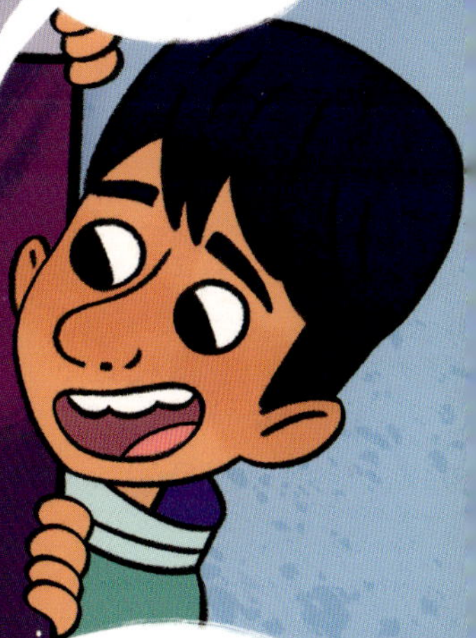

**Venus** is **EVEN hotter** than **Mercury,** even though it's farther away from the sun, because it has an **atmosphere** to keep it warm.

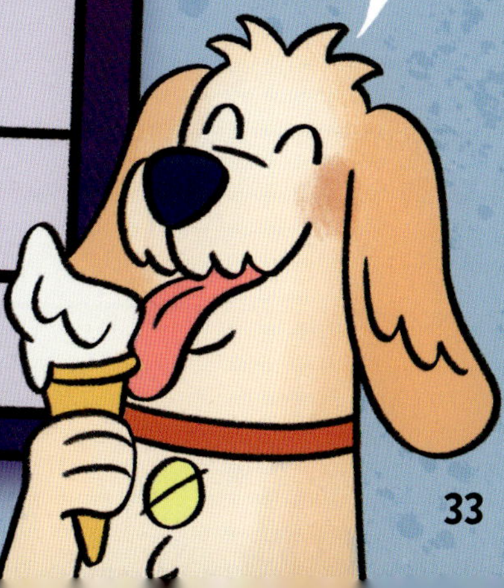

# EARTH

## THE NAME COMES FROM AN ANCIENT WORD MEANING GROUND OR SOIL

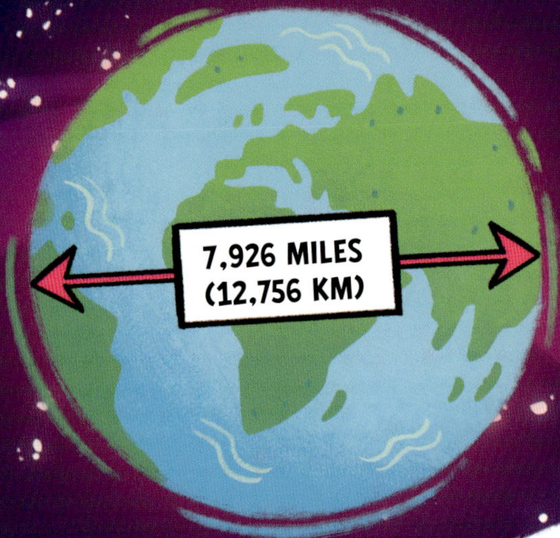
7,926 MILES
(12,756 KM)

The only planet that supports life—as far as we know!

The time it takes to spin around once (one day): 24 HOURS

The time it takes to orbit the sun (one year): 365 DAYS

Protected by an atmosphere (which keeps us warm) and a magnetic field (which shields us from the sun's radiation)

Moons: 1

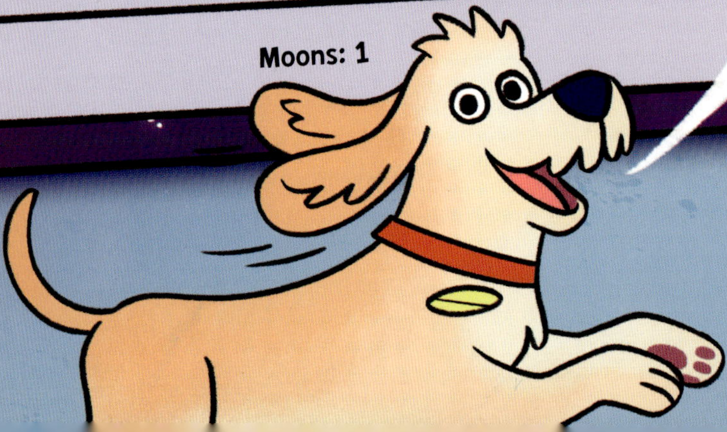
These numbers are approximate (the same as for all the other planets)—**one year is 365** and a quarter days, and that's why we have **leap years!**

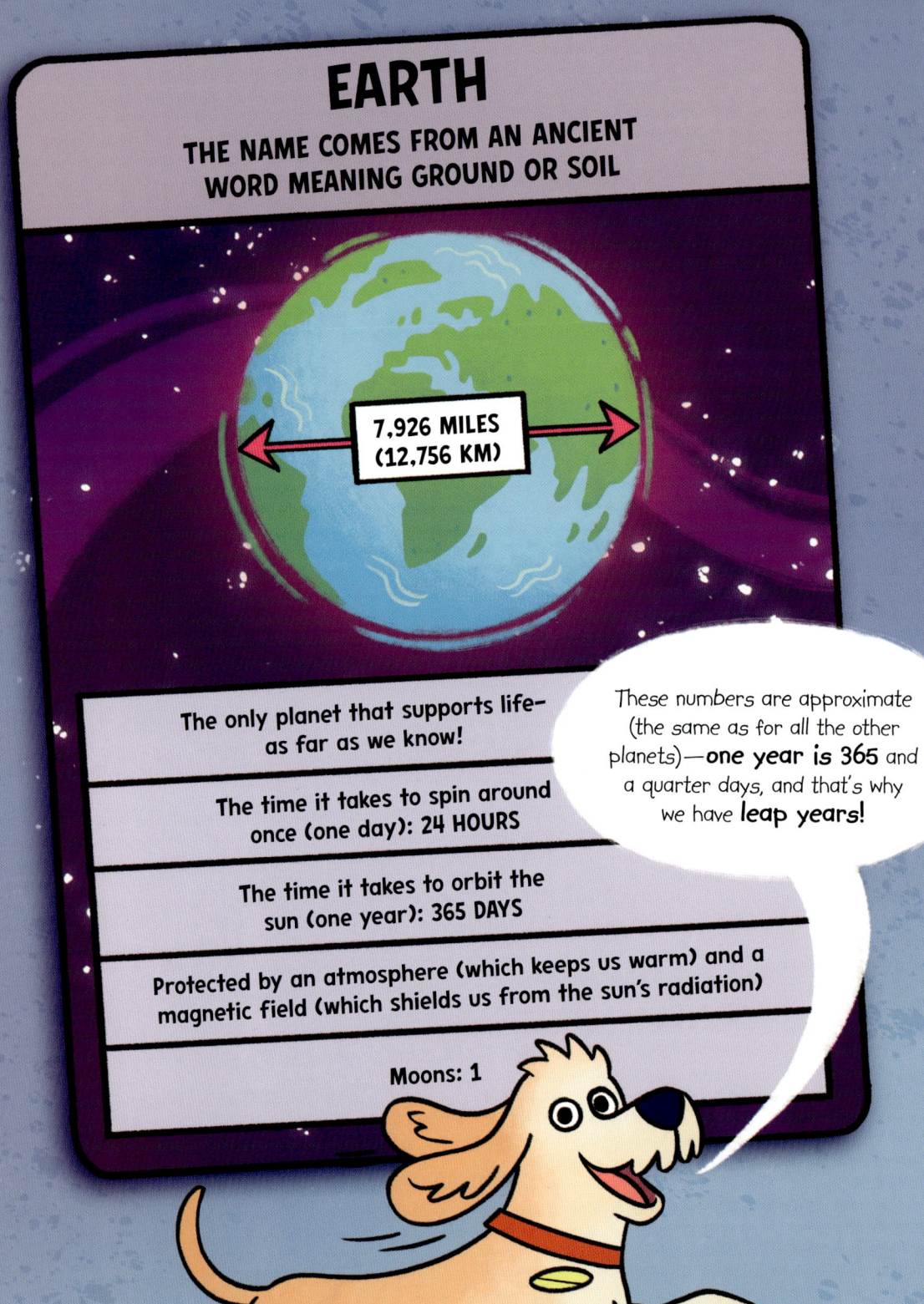

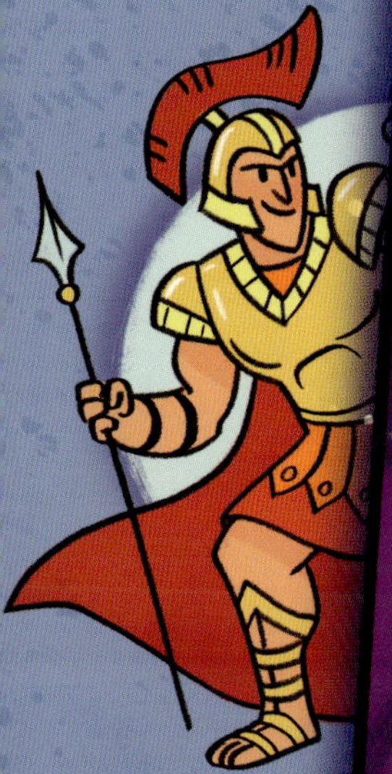

# MARS

## NAMED AFTER THE ANCIENT ROMAN GOD OF WAR

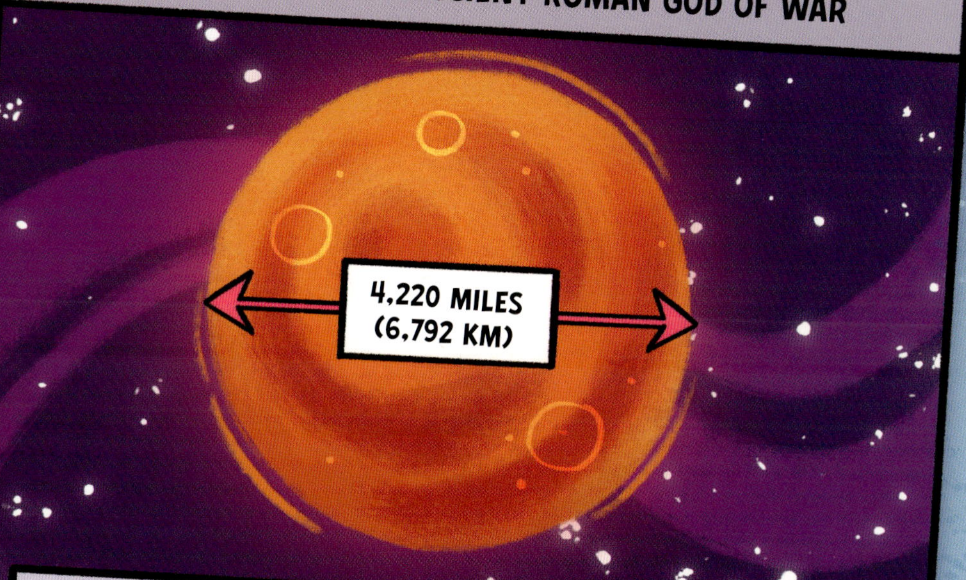
4,220 MILES
(6,792 KM)

Mars appears red because its soil contains iron oxide (rust).

The time it takes to spin around once (one Mars day): 25 HOURS

The time it takes to orbit the sun (one Mars year): 687 DAYS

Mercury, Venus, Earth, and Mars are known as the inner planets.

Moons: 2

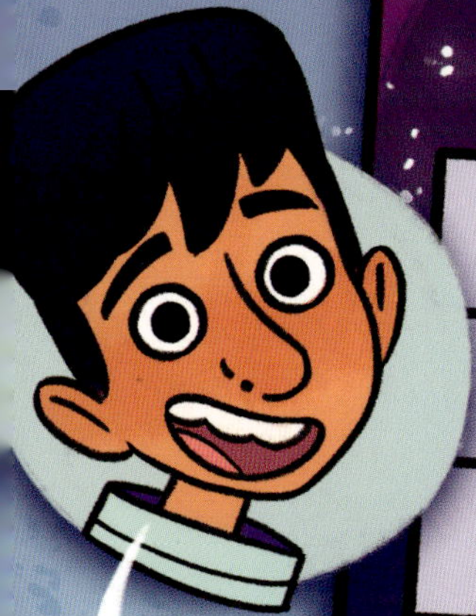
Mars has **two potato-shaped** moons called **Phobos** (which means **fear**) and **Deimos** (which means **dread**)

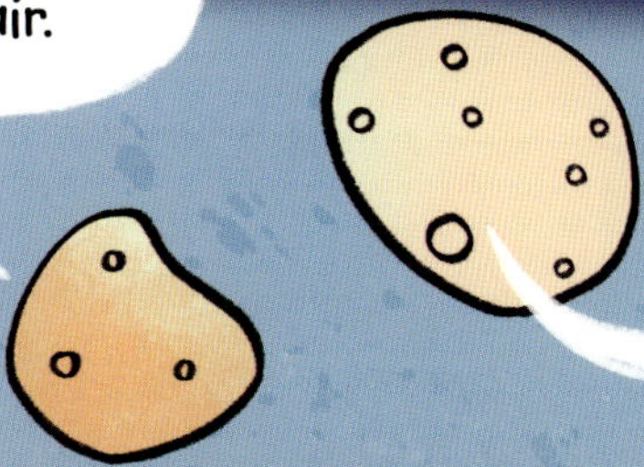
That's a little **unfair.**
We're **lovely** when you get to **know us!**

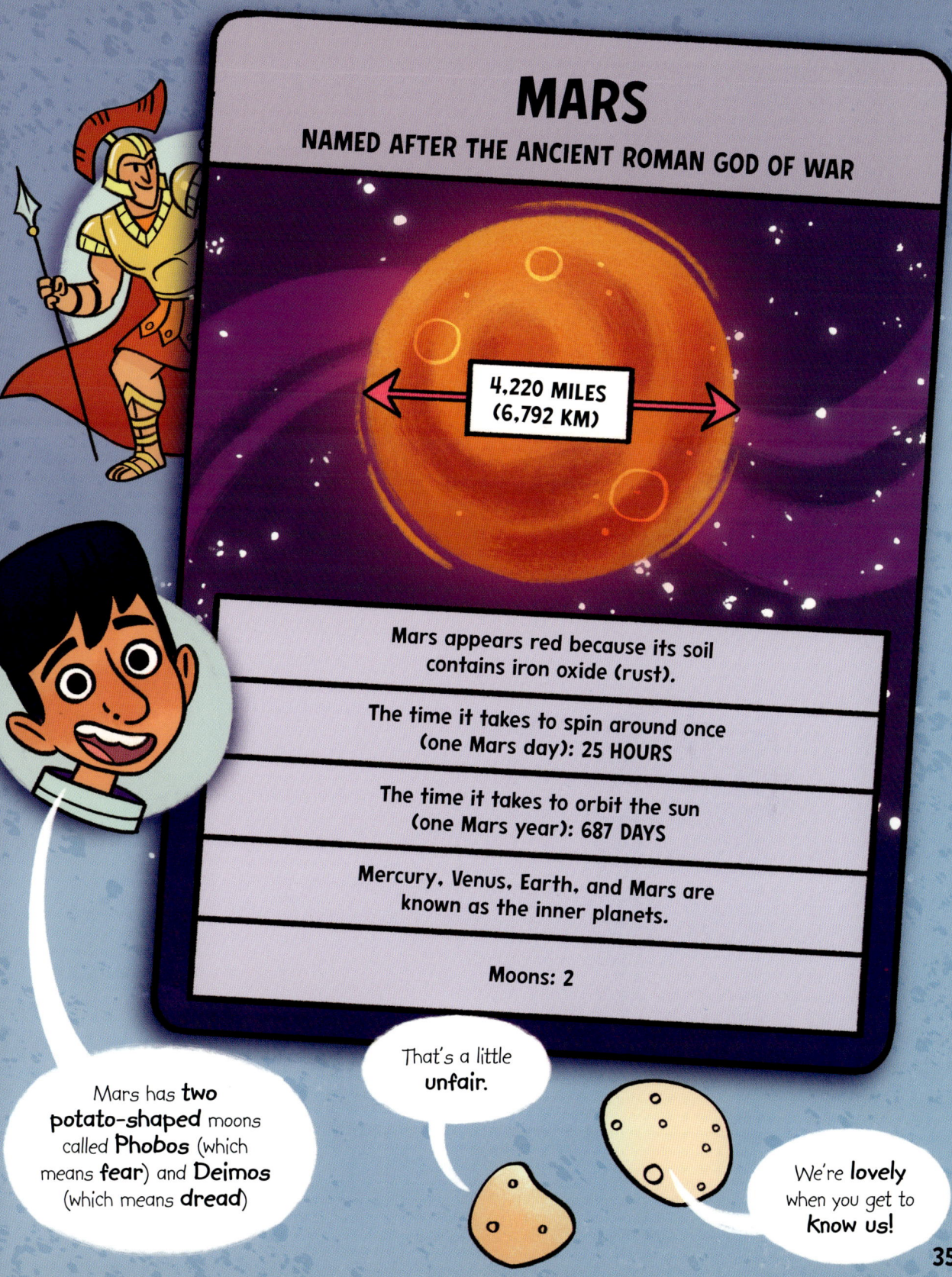

# JUPITER

## NAMED AFTER THE ANCIENT ROMAN KING OF THE GODS

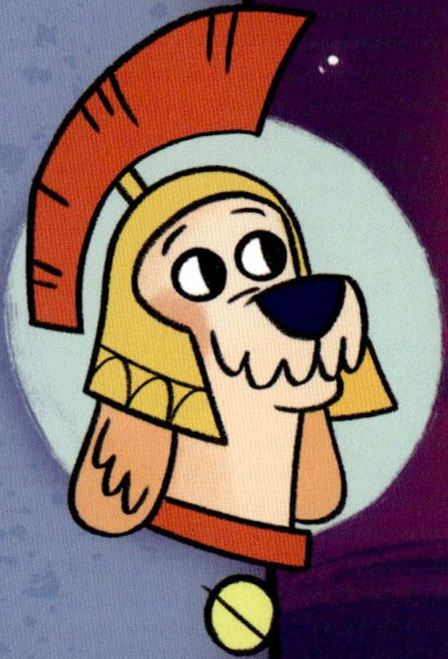

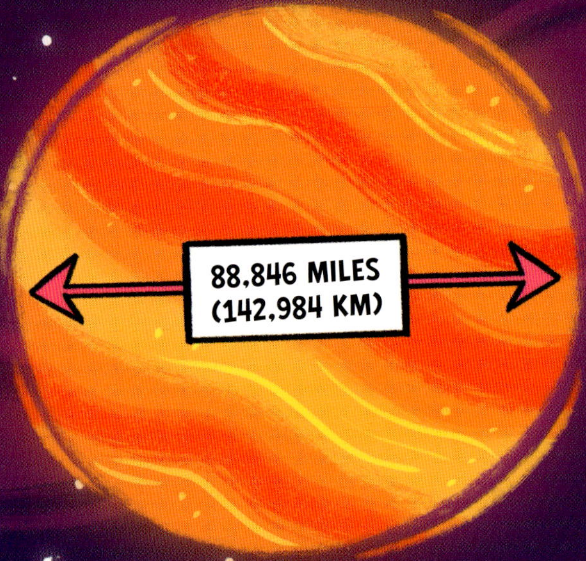
88,846 MILES
(142,984 KM)

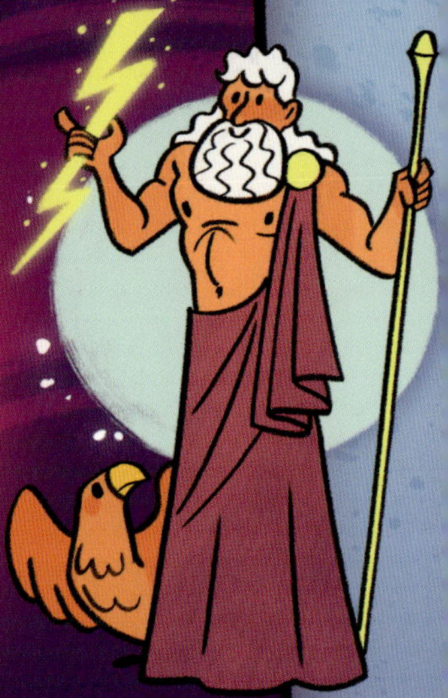

| |
|---|
| Biggest planet in the solar system |
| The time it takes to spin around once (one Jupiter day): 10 HOURS (the shortest in the solar system) |
| The time it takes to orbit the sun (one Jupiter year): 4,333 DAYS |
| Moons: AT LEAST 95 |

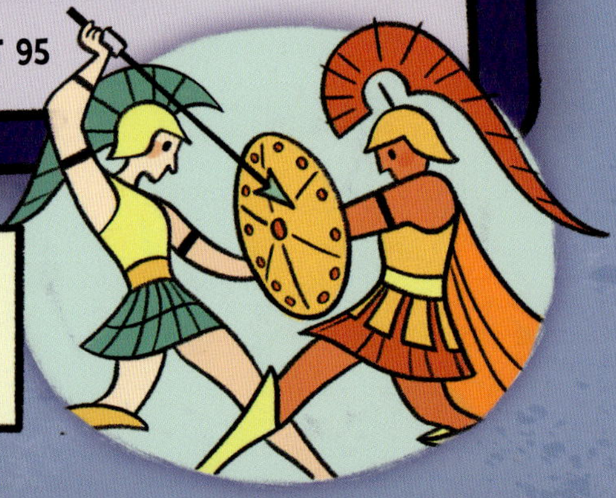

Asteroids, called Greeks and Trojans (named after opposing sides in a war from Greek mythology), accompany Jupiter in orbit.

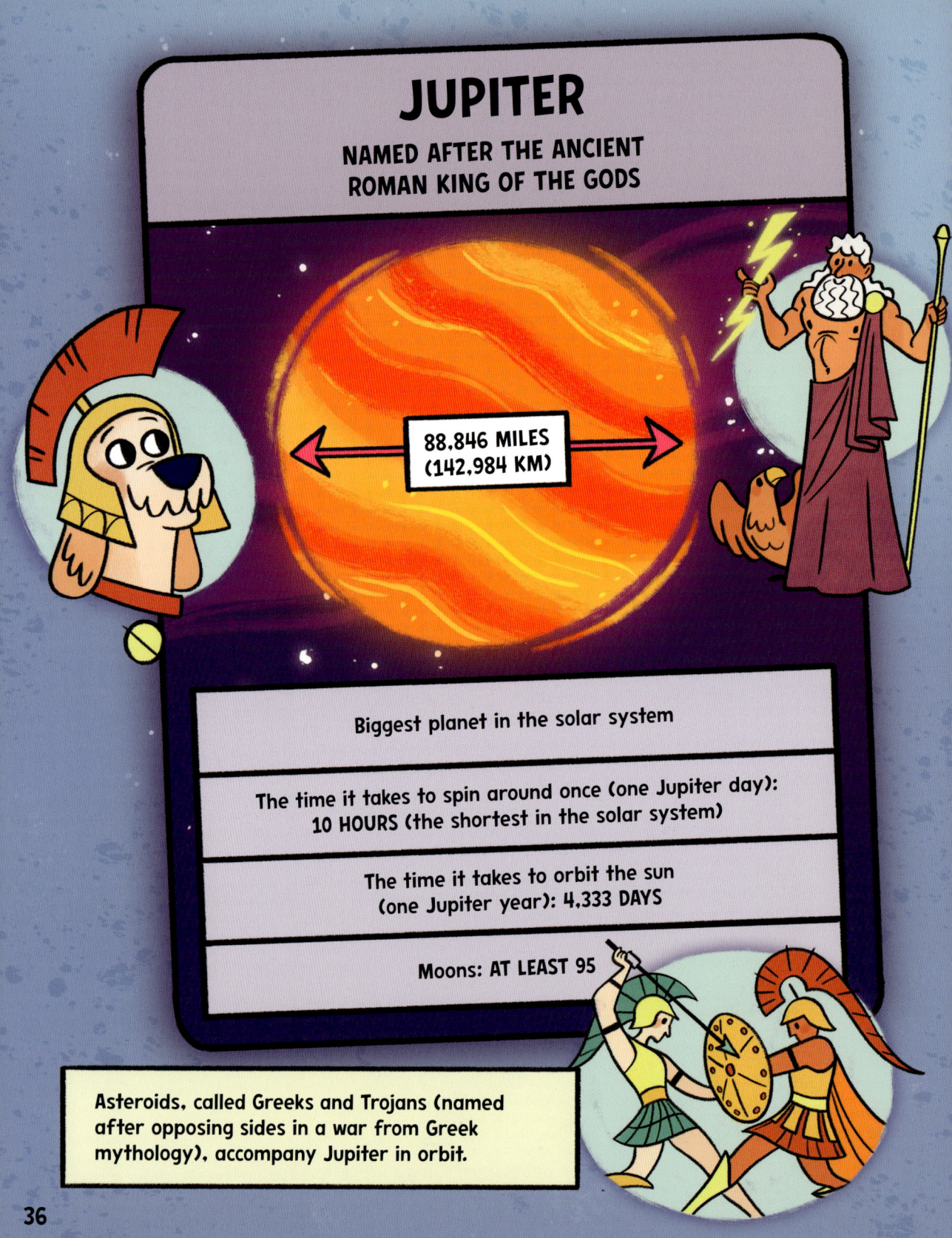

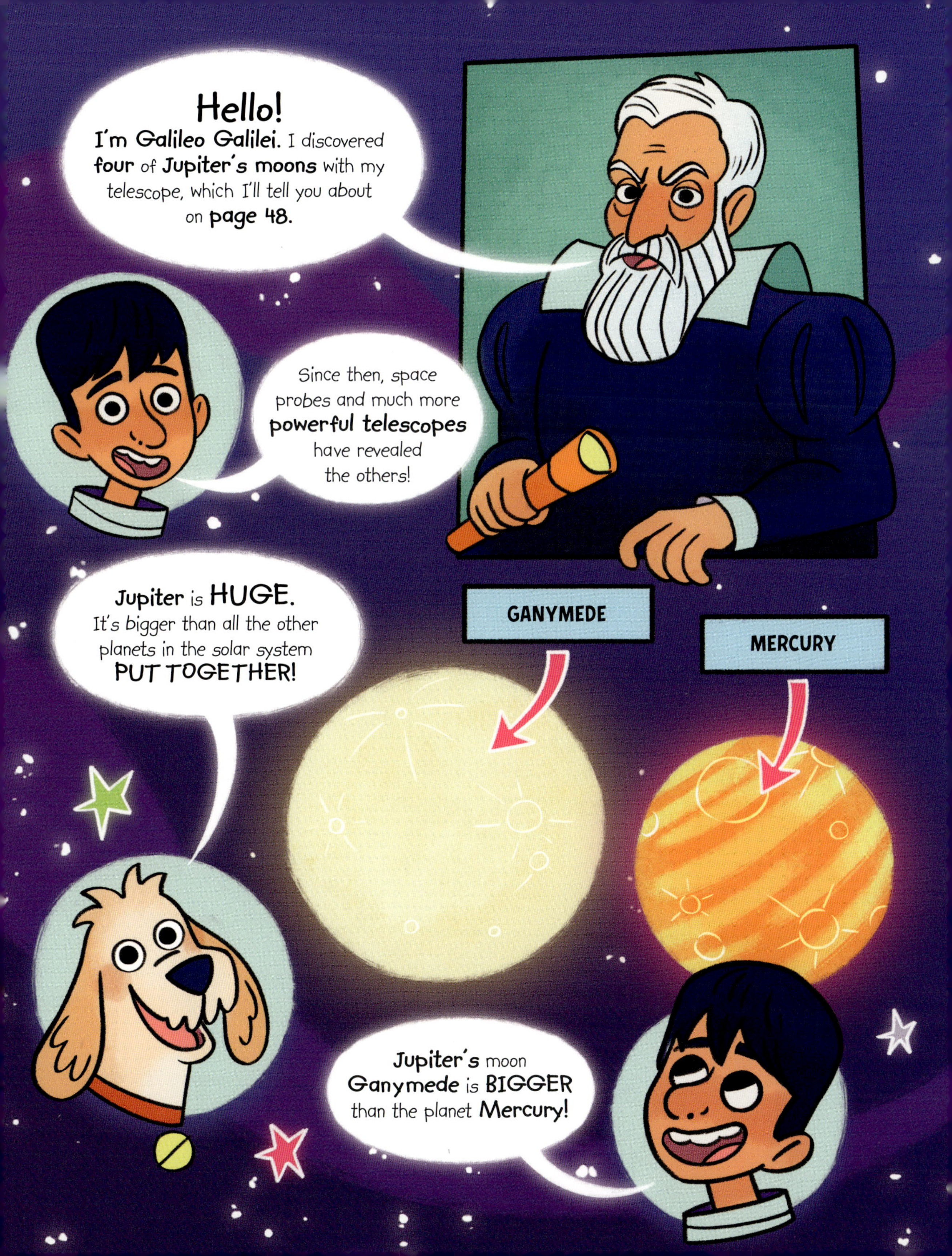
Hello!
I'm Galileo Galilei. I discovered four of Jupiter's moons with my telescope, which I'll tell you about on page 48.
Since then, space probes and much more powerful telescopes have revealed the others!
Jupiter is HUGE. It's bigger than all the other planets in the solar system PUT TOGETHER!
GANYMEDE
MERCURY
Jupiter's moon Ganymede is BIGGER than the planet Mercury!

# SATURN

## NAMED AFTER THE ANCIENT ROMAN GOD OF FARMING

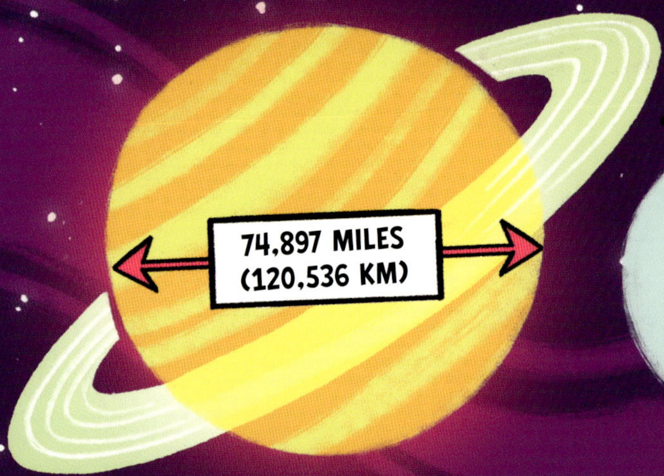
74,897 MILES
(120,536 KM)

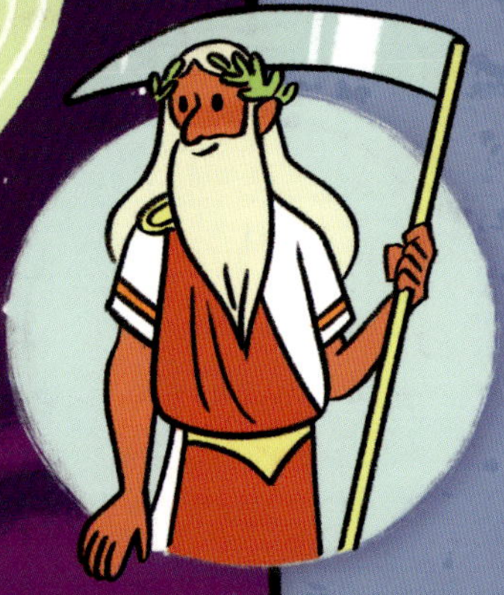

The second-largest planet in the solar system

The time it takes to spin around once (one Saturn day): 11 HOURS

The time it takes to orbit the sun (one Saturn year): 10,759 DAYS

Saturn's biggest moon, Titan, has a thick atmosphere and some scientists think there might be life there.

Moons: MORE THAN 140

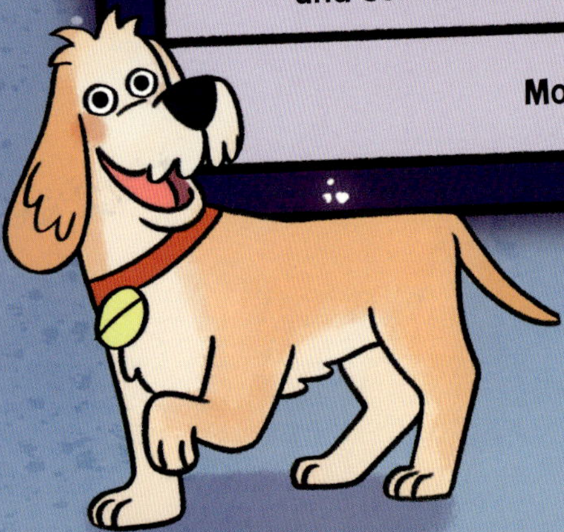

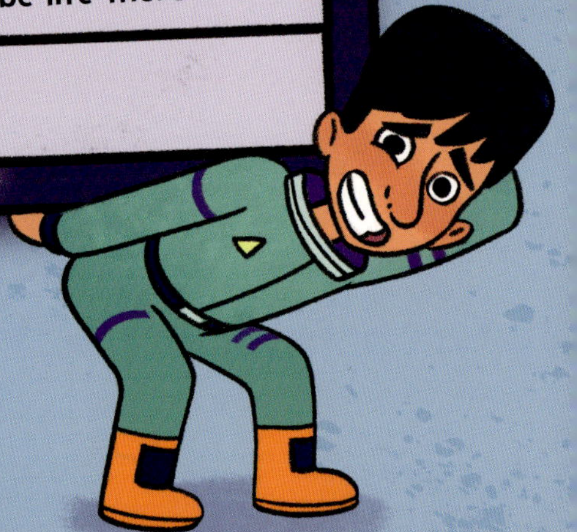

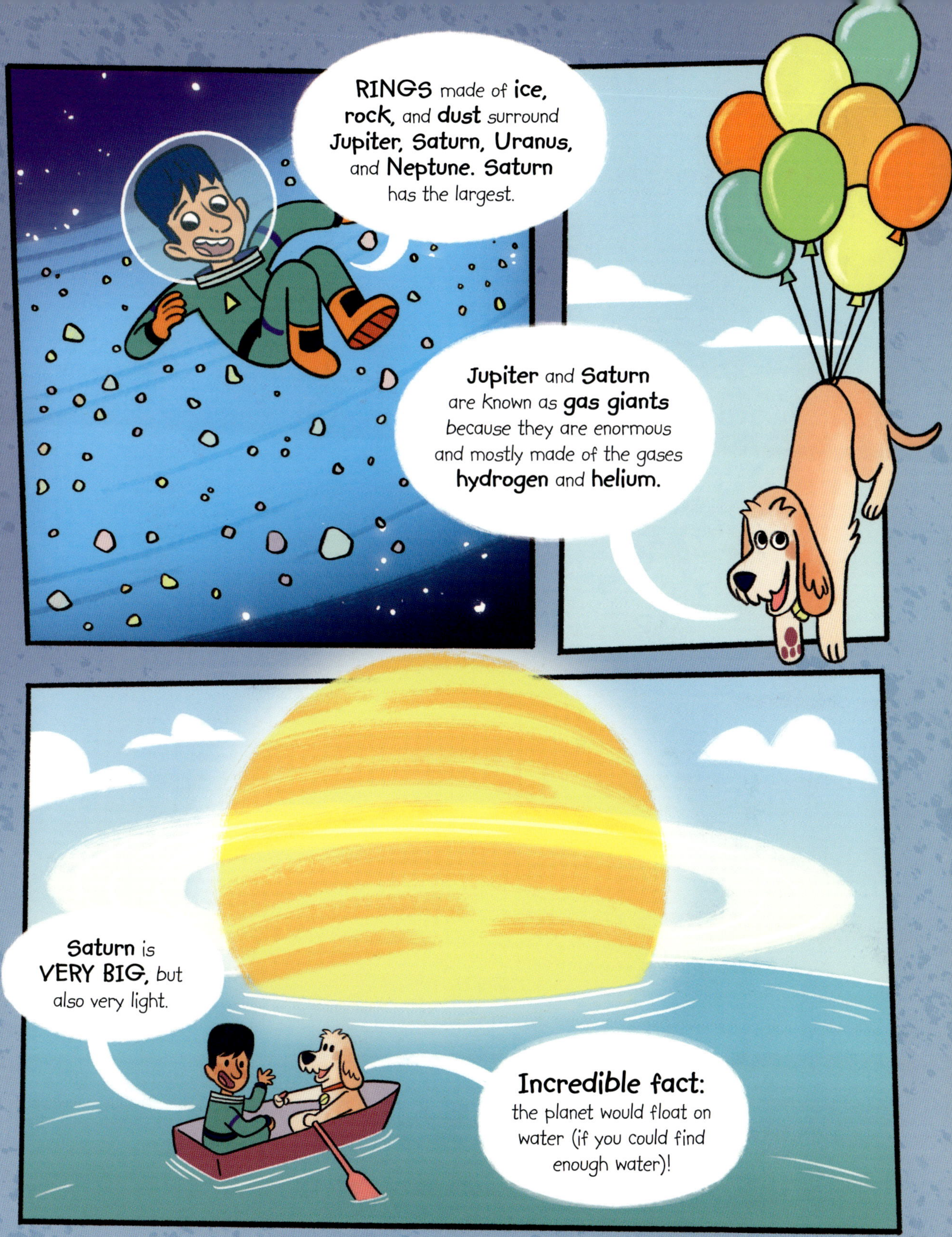
RINGS made of ice, rock, and dust surround Jupiter, Saturn, Uranus, and Neptune. Saturn has the largest.
Jupiter and Saturn are known as gas giants because they are enormous and mostly made of the gases hydrogen and helium.
Saturn is VERY BIG, but also very light.
Incredible fact: the planet would float on water (if you could find enough water)!

# URANUS

**NAMED AFTER THE ANCIENT ROMAN GOD OF THE SKY**

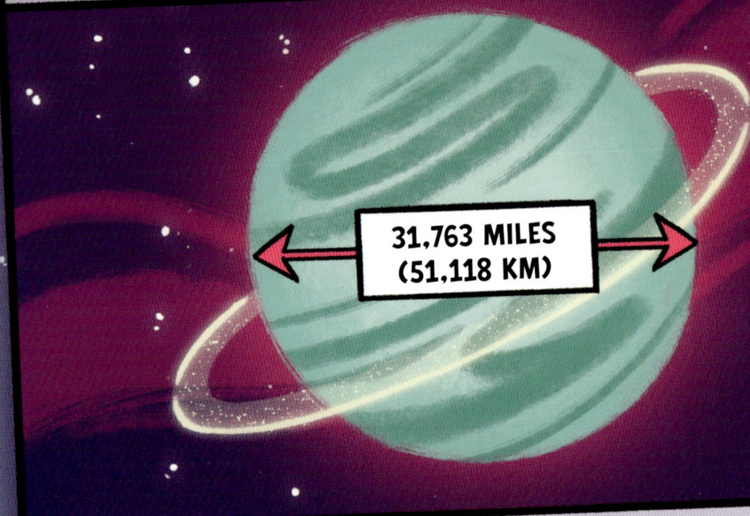
31,763 MILES
(51,118 KM)

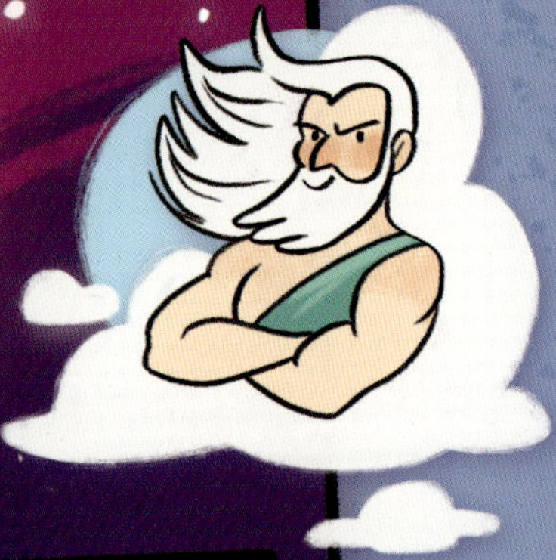

| |
|---|
| Spins on its side, unlike all the other planets in the solar system |
| The time it takes to spin around once (one Uranus day): 17 HOURS |
| The time it takes to orbit the sun (one Uranus year): 30,688 DAYS |
| Rings made of ice, rocks, and dust |
| Moons: AT LEAST 28 |

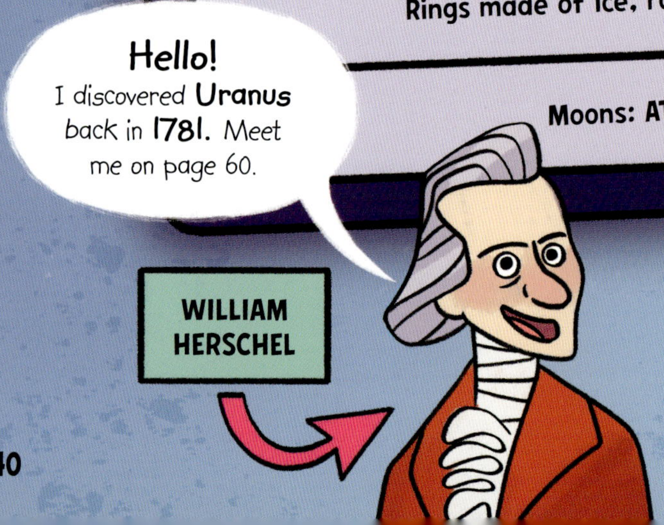
Hello! I discovered Uranus back in 1781. Meet me on page 60.
WILLIAM HERSCHEL

William Herschel didn't spot that Uranus has rings, which were first seen in 1977 with a much more powerful telescope than Herschel's.

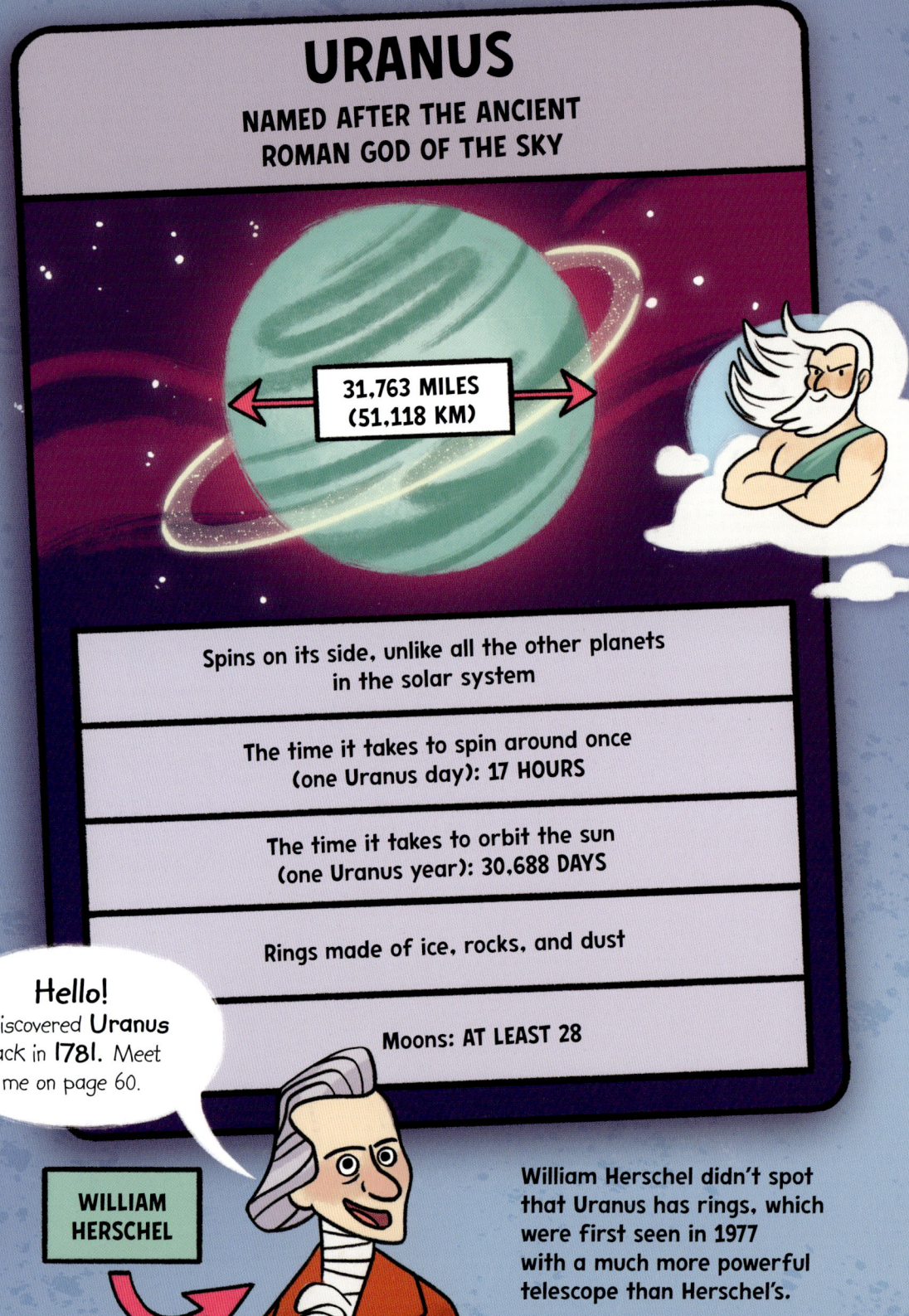

# NEPTUNE

## NAMED AFTER THE ANCIENT ROMAN GOD OF THE SEA

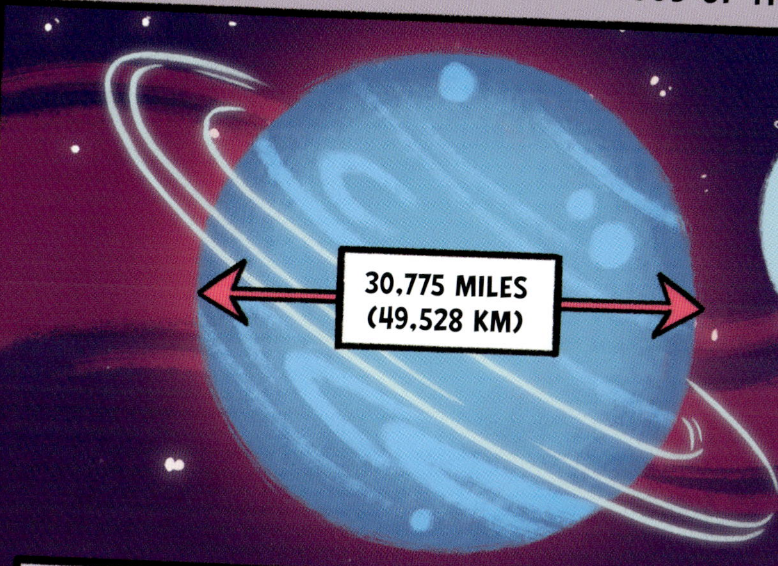
30,775 MILES
(49,528 KM)

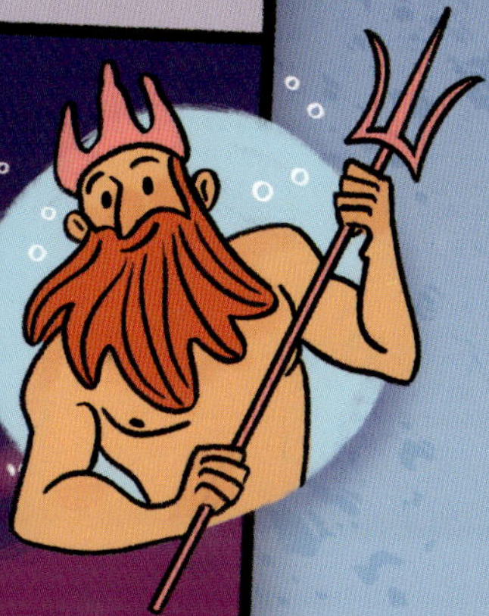

The time it takes to orbit the sun (one Neptune year): 60,195 DAYS (a year lasts a very long time on these faraway planets—this is about 164 Earth years)

The time it takes to spin around once (one Neptune day): 16 HOURS

Fastest winds in the solar system

Moons: 14

MATHEMATICIANS JOHN COUCH ADAMS AND URBAIN JEAN JOSEPH LE VERRIER

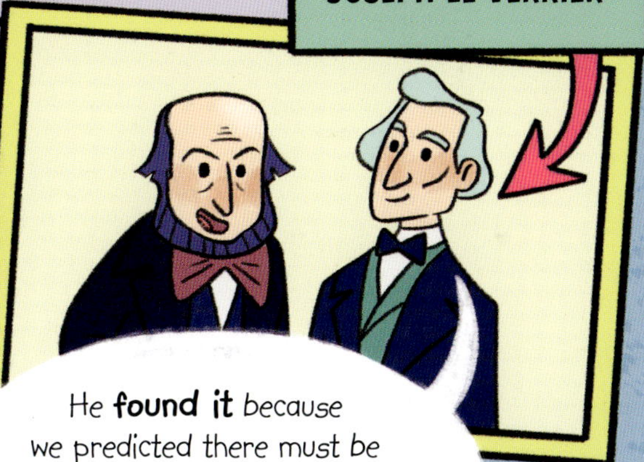

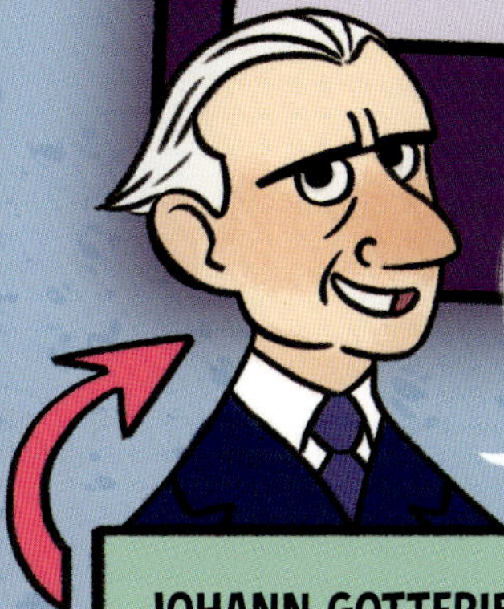

I was the **FIRST** to identify the planet **Neptune** in **1846**!

JOHANN GOTTFRIED GALLE

He **found it** because we predicted there must be another planet **pulling Uranus** from its **orbit**. We even said **where** it was and **how big** it was!

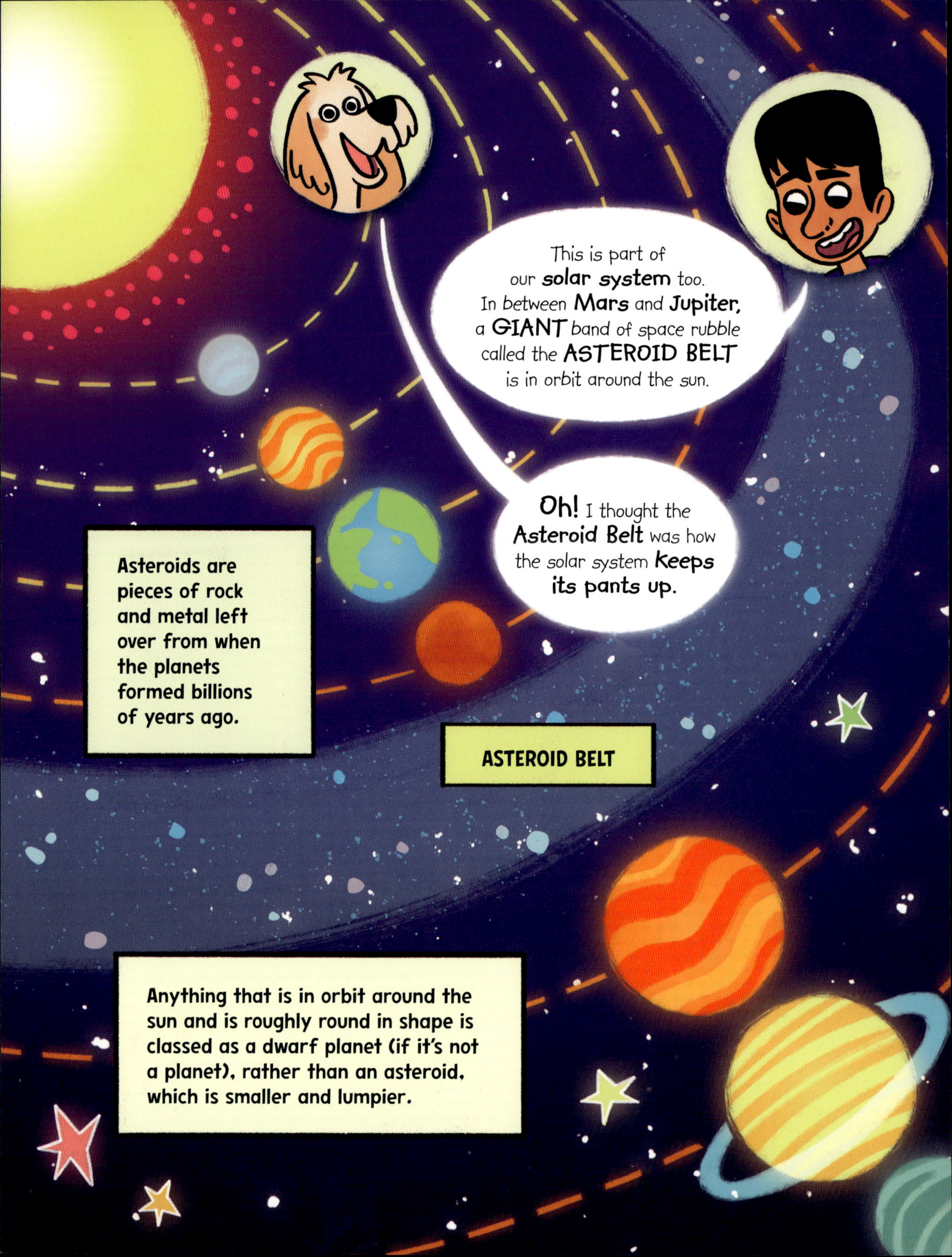
This is part of our **solar system** too. In between **Mars** and **Jupiter**, a **GIANT** band of space rubble called the **ASTEROID BELT** is in orbit around the sun.
**Oh!** I thought the **Asteroid Belt** was how the solar system **keeps its pants up.**
Asteroids are pieces of rock and metal left over from when the planets formed billions of years ago.
ASTEROID BELT
Anything that is in orbit around the sun and is roughly round in shape is classed as a dwarf planet (if it's not a planet), rather than an asteroid, which is smaller and lumpier.

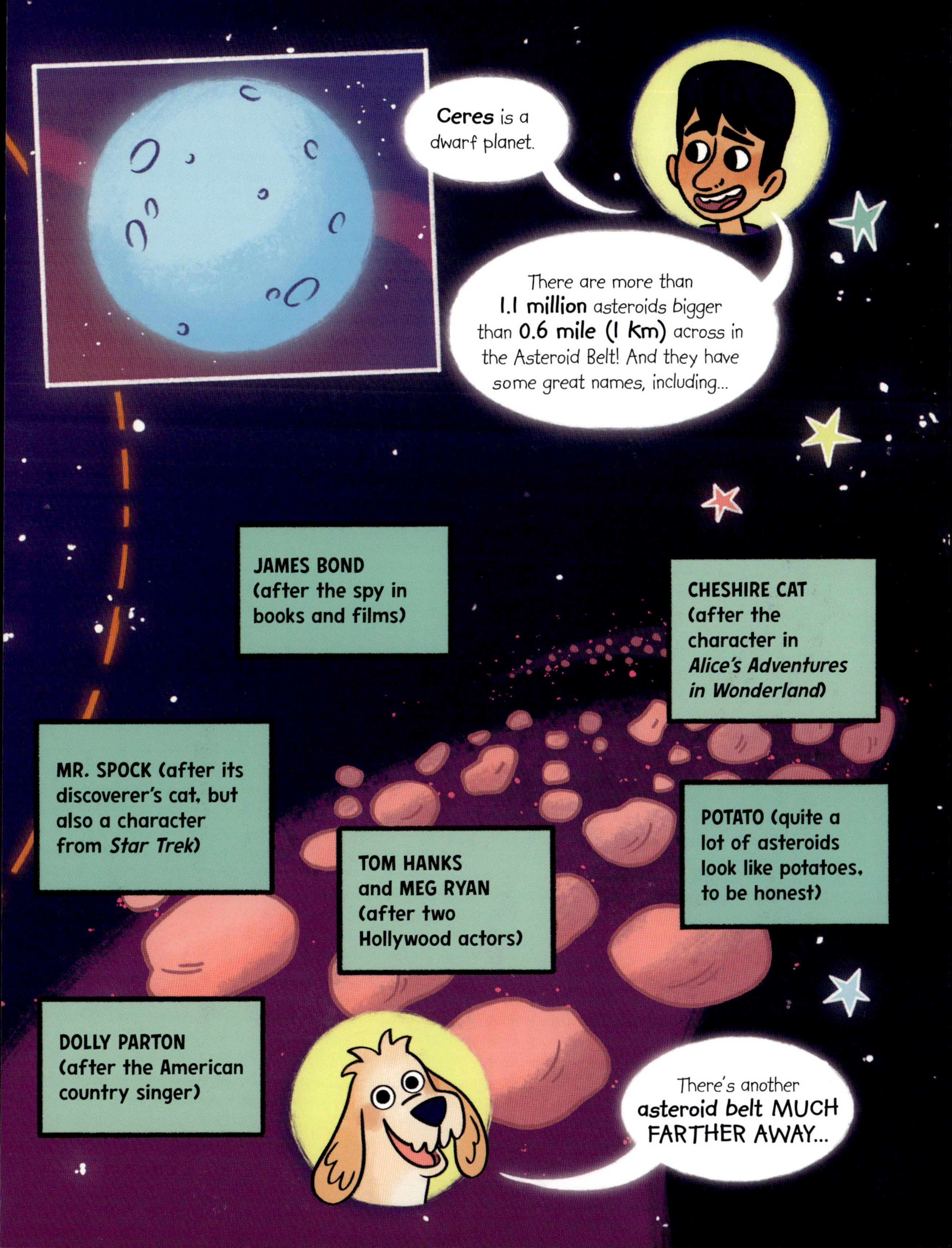

**Ceres** is a dwarf planet.
There are more than **1.1 million** asteroids bigger than **0.6 mile (1 km)** across in the Asteroid Belt! And they have some great names, including...
**JAMES BOND (after the spy in books and films)**
**CHESHIRE CAT (after the character in *Alice's Adventures in Wonderland*)**
**MR. SPOCK (after its discoverer's cat, but also a character from *Star Trek*)**
**TOM HANKS and MEG RYAN (after two Hollywood actors)**
**POTATO (quite a lot of asteroids look like potatoes, to be honest)**
**DOLLY PARTON (after the American country singer)**
There's another **asteroid belt** MUCH FARTHER AWAY...

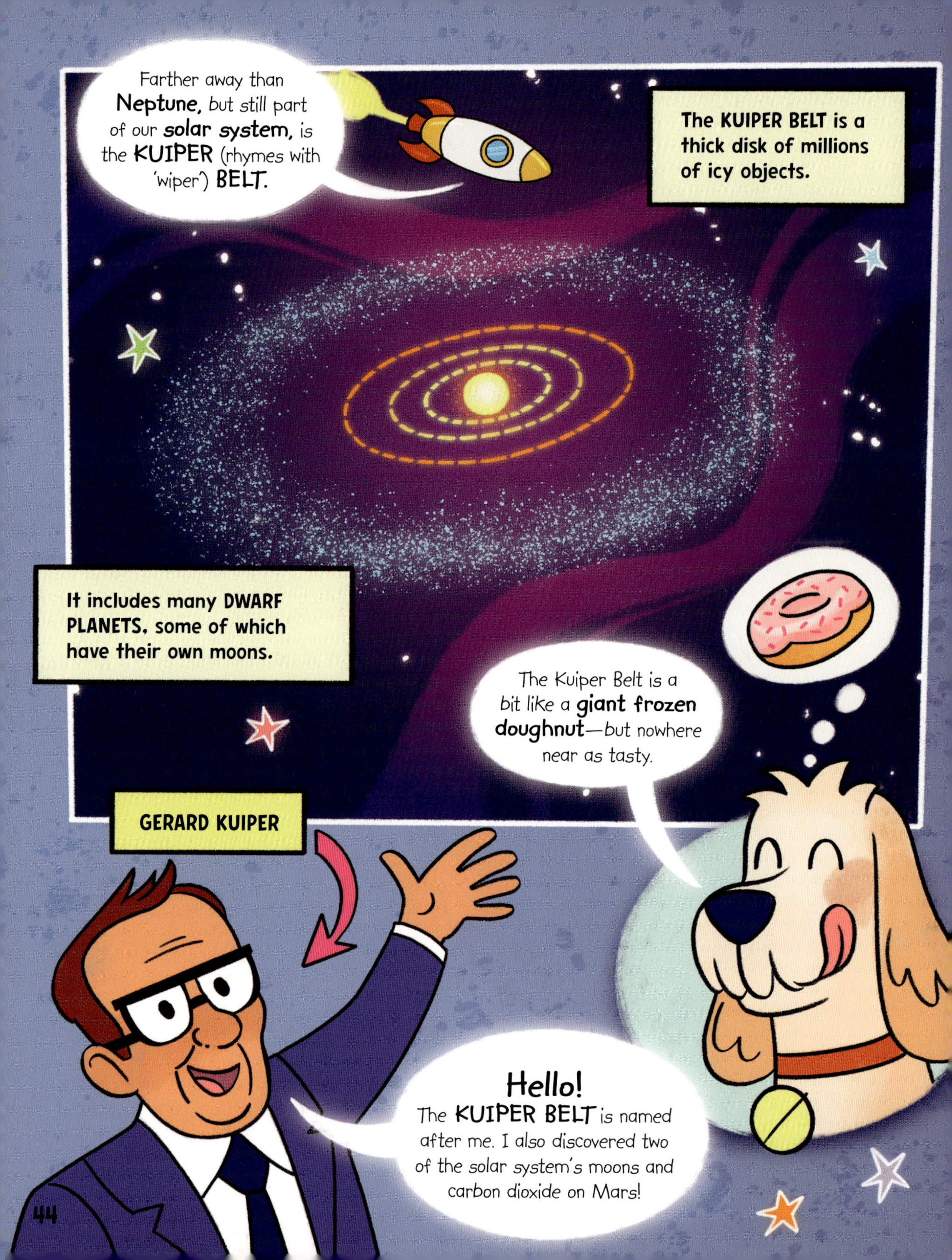

Farther away than Neptune, but still part of our solar system, is the KUIPER (rhymes with 'wiper') BELT.
The KUIPER BELT is a thick disk of millions of icy objects.
It includes many DWARF PLANETS, some of which have their own moons.
The Kuiper Belt is a bit like a giant frozen doughnut—but nowhere near as tasty.
GERARD KUIPER
Hello!
The KUIPER BELT is named after me. I also discovered two of the solar system's moons and carbon dioxide on Mars!

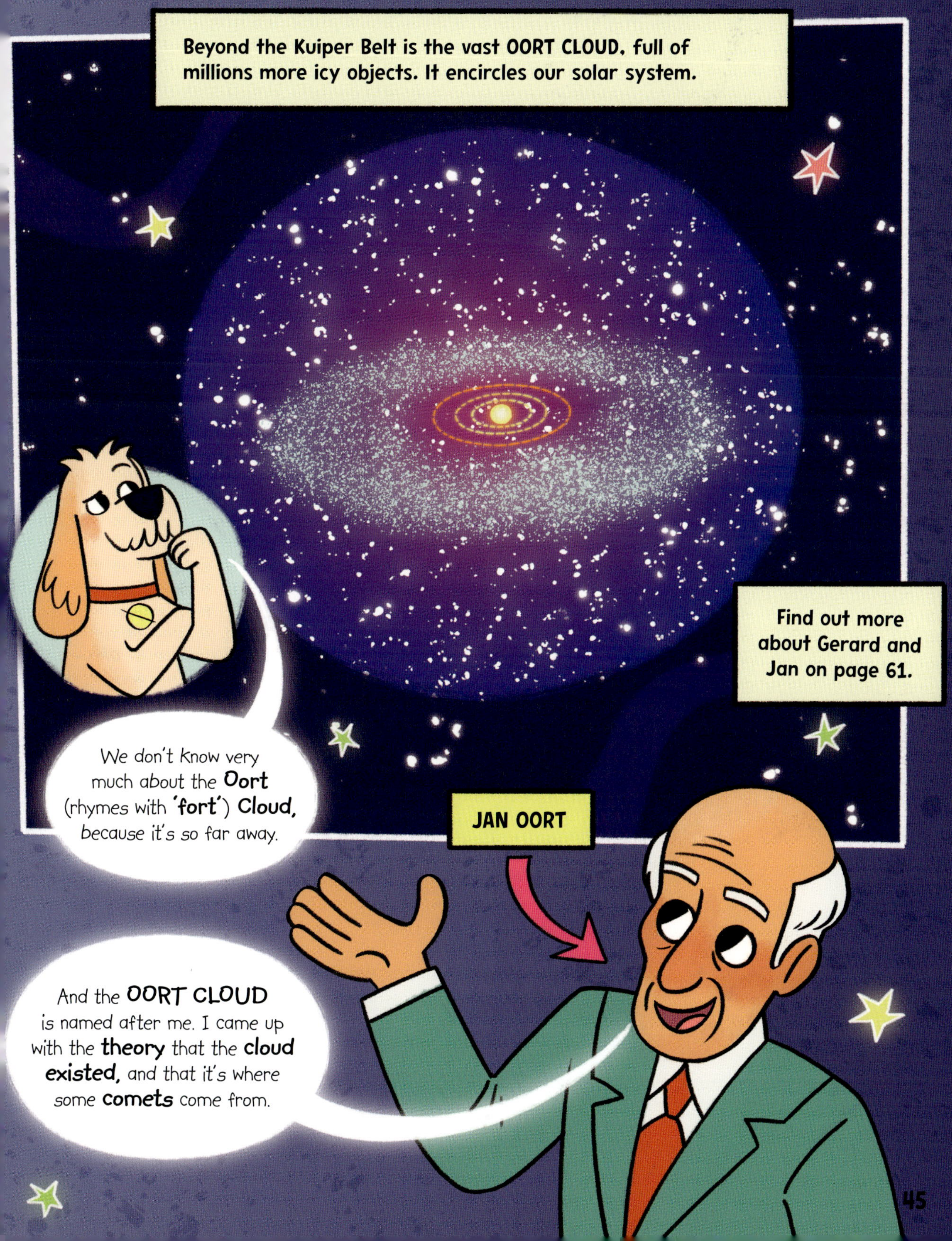

Beyond the Kuiper Belt is the vast OORT CLOUD, full of millions more icy objects. It encircles our solar system.
Find out more about Gerard and Jan on page 61.
We don't know very much about the Oort (rhymes with 'fort') Cloud, because it's so far away.
JAN OORT
And the OORT CLOUD is named after me. I came up with the theory that the cloud existed, and that it's where some comets come from.

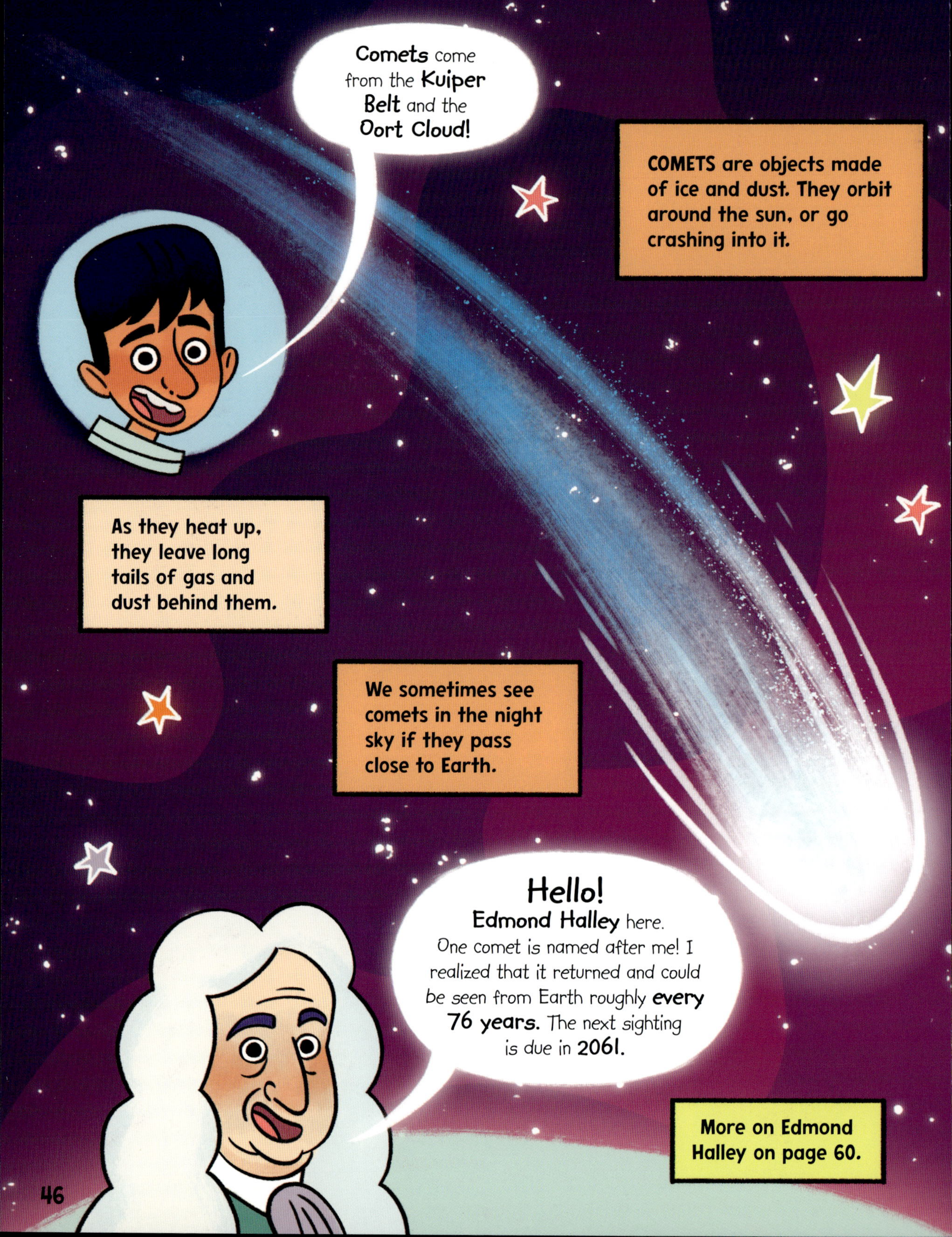

Comets come from the Kuiper Belt and the Oort Cloud!
COMETS are objects made of ice and dust. They orbit around the sun, or go crashing into it.
As they heat up, they leave long tails of gas and dust behind them.
We sometimes see comets in the night sky if they pass close to Earth.
Hello! Edmond Halley here. One comet is named after me! I realized that it returned and could be seen from Earth roughly every 76 years. The next sighting is due in 2061.
More on Edmond Halley on page 60.

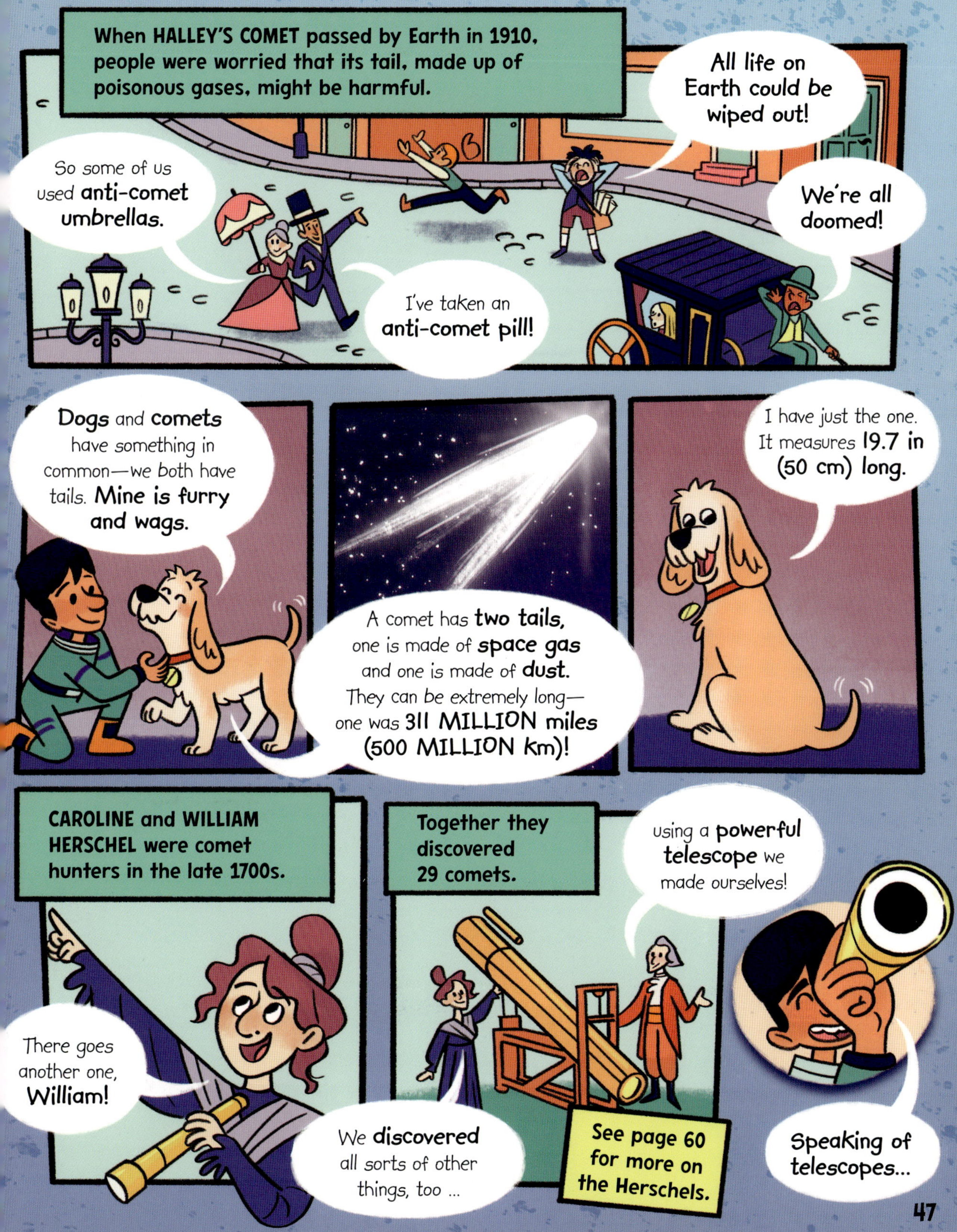

When HALLEY'S COMET passed by Earth in 1910, people were worried that its tail, made up of poisonous gases, might be harmful.
So some of us used anti-comet umbrellas.
I've taken an anti-comet pill!
All life on Earth could be wiped out!
We're all doomed!
Dogs and comets have something in common—we both have tails. Mine is furry and wags.
A comet has two tails, one is made of space gas and one is made of dust. They can be extremely long—one was 311 MILLION miles (500 MILLION km)!
I have just the one. It measures 19.7 in (50 cm) long.
CAROLINE and WILLIAM HERSCHEL were comet hunters in the late 1700s.
There goes another one, William!
We discovered all sorts of other things, too ...
Together they discovered 29 comets.
using a powerful telescope we made ourselves!
See page 60 for more on the Herschels.
Speaking of telescopes...

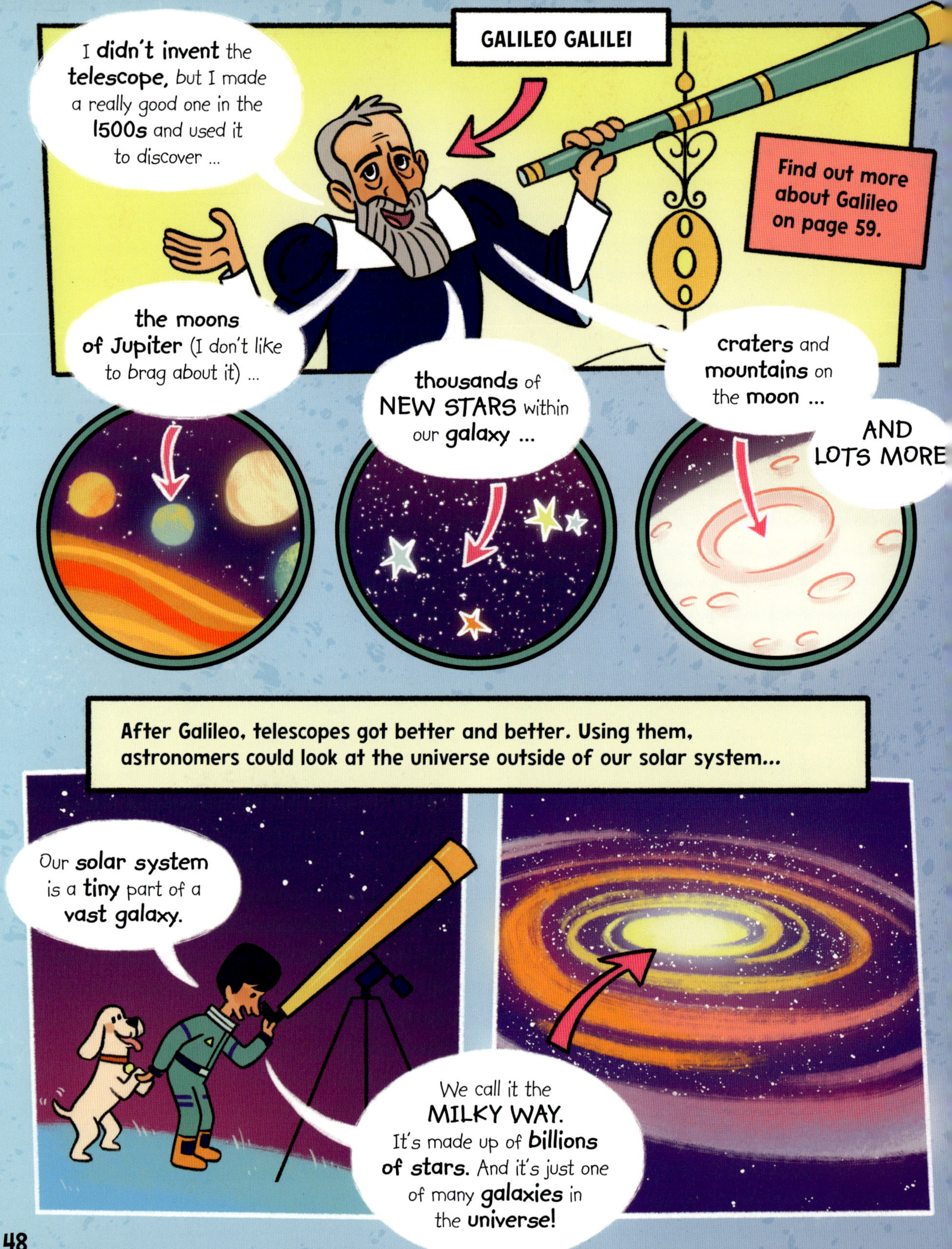
GALILEO GALILEI
I didn't invent the telescope, but I made a really good one in the 1500s and used it to discover ...
Find out more about Galileo on page 59.
the moons of Jupiter (I don't like to brag about it) ...
thousands of NEW STARS within our galaxy ...
craters and mountains on the moon ...
AND LOTS MORE
After Galileo, telescopes got better and better. Using them, astronomers could look at the universe outside of our solar system...
Our solar system is a tiny part of a vast galaxy.
We call it the MILKY WAY. It's made up of billions of stars. And it's just one of many galaxies in the universe!

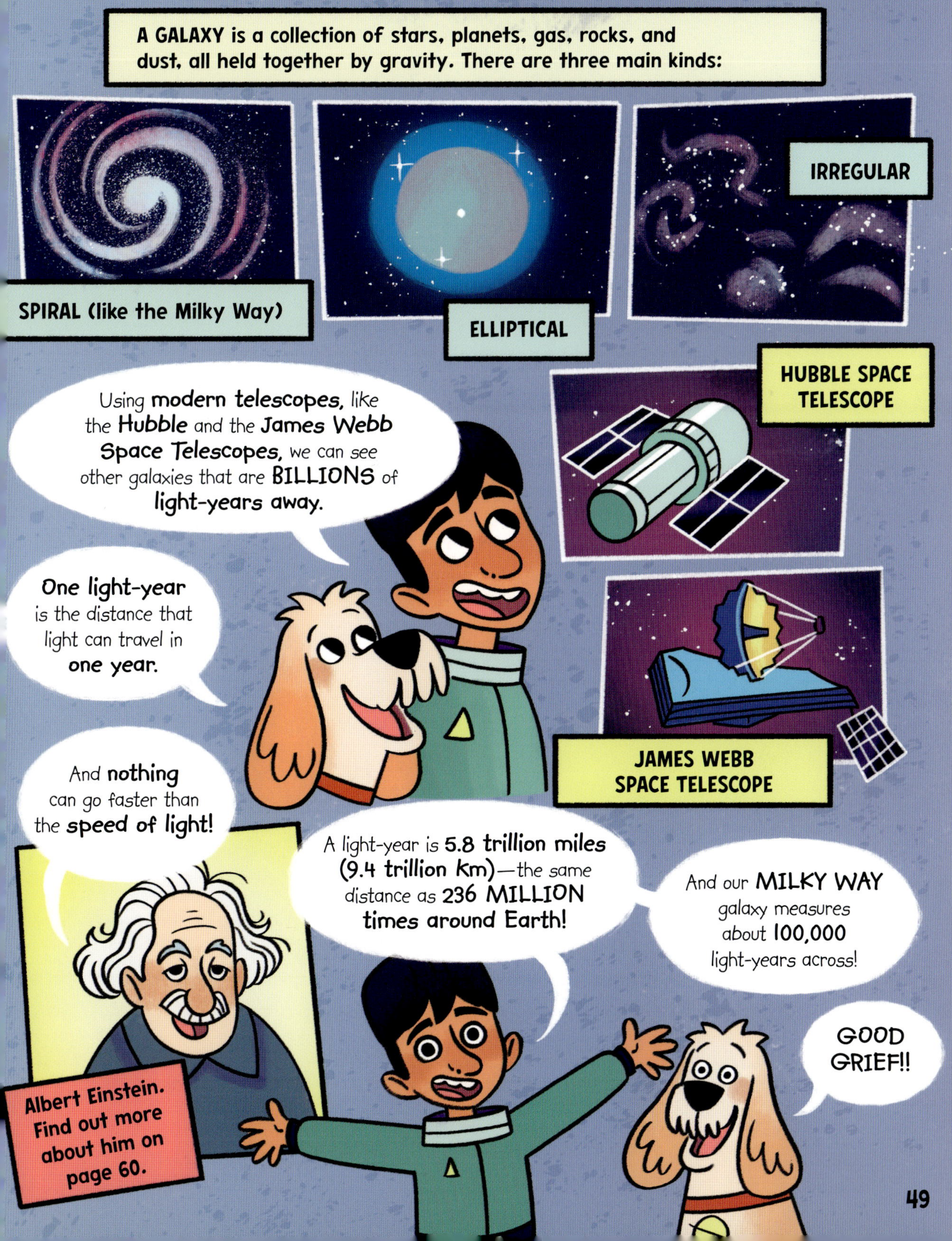
A GALAXY is a collection of stars, planets, gas, rocks, and dust, all held together by gravity. There are three main kinds:
SPIRAL (like the Milky Way)
ELLIPTICAL
IRREGULAR
Using modern telescopes, like the Hubble and the James Webb Space Telescopes, we can see other galaxies that are BILLIONS of light-years away.
HUBBLE SPACE TELESCOPE
One light-year is the distance that light can travel in one year.
JAMES WEBB SPACE TELESCOPE
And nothing can go faster than the speed of light!
A light-year is 5.8 trillion miles (9.4 trillion km)—the same distance as 236 MILLION times around Earth!
And our MILKY WAY galaxy measures about 100,000 light-years across!
Albert Einstein. Find out more about him on page 60.
GOOD GRIEF!!

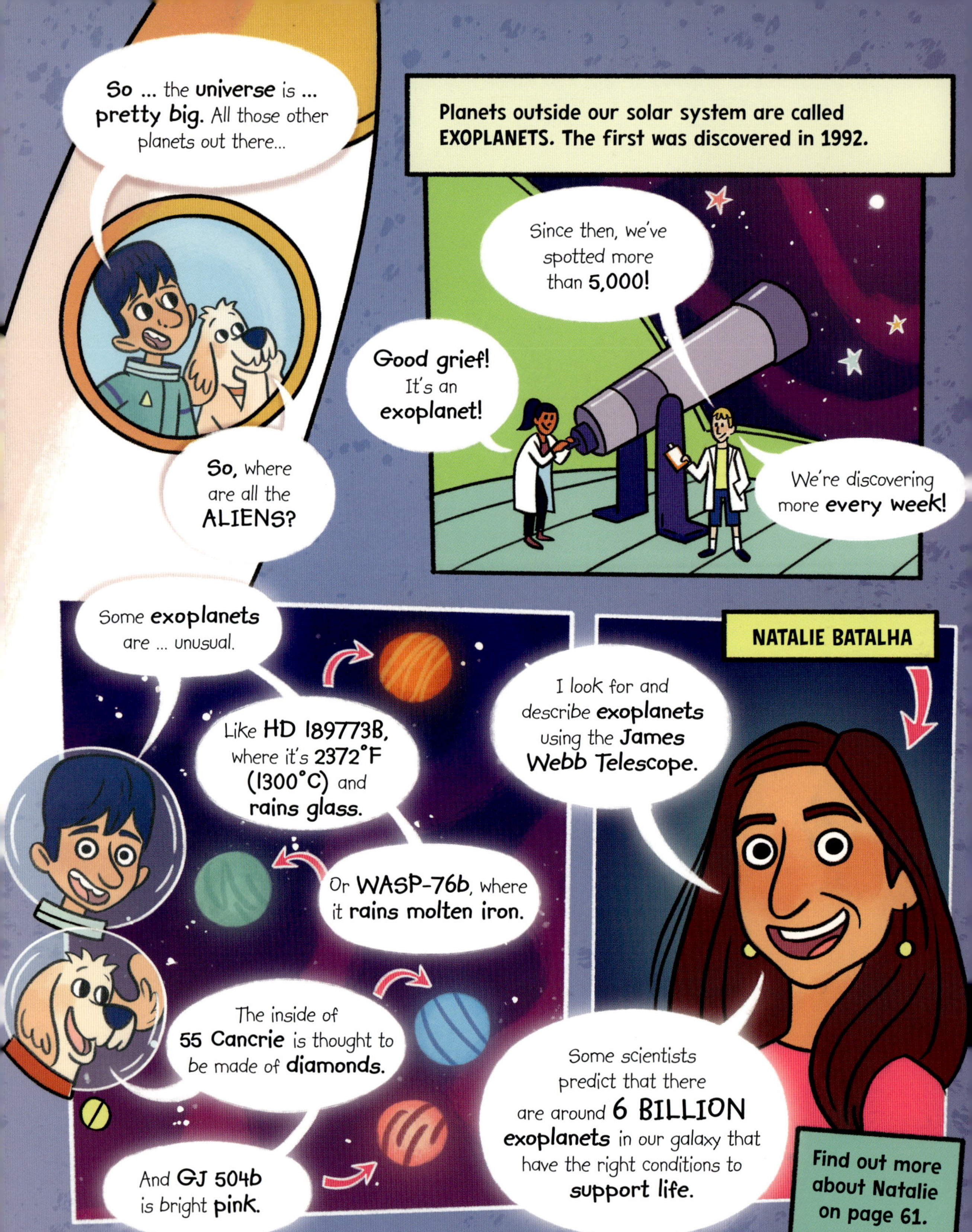
So ... the universe is ... pretty big. All those other planets out there...
So, where are all the ALIENS?
Planets outside our solar system are called EXOPLANETS. The first was discovered in 1992.
Since then, we've spotted more than 5,000!
Good grief! It's an exoplanet!
We're discovering more every week!
Some exoplanets are ... unusual.
Like HD 189773B, where it's 2372°F (1300°C) and rains glass.
Or WASP-76b, where it rains molten iron.
The inside of 55 Cancrie is thought to be made of diamonds.
And GJ 504b is bright pink.
NATALIE BATALHA
I look for and describe exoplanets using the James Webb Telescope.
Some scientists predict that there are around 6 BILLION exoplanets in our galaxy that have the right conditions to support life.
Find out more about Natalie on page 61.

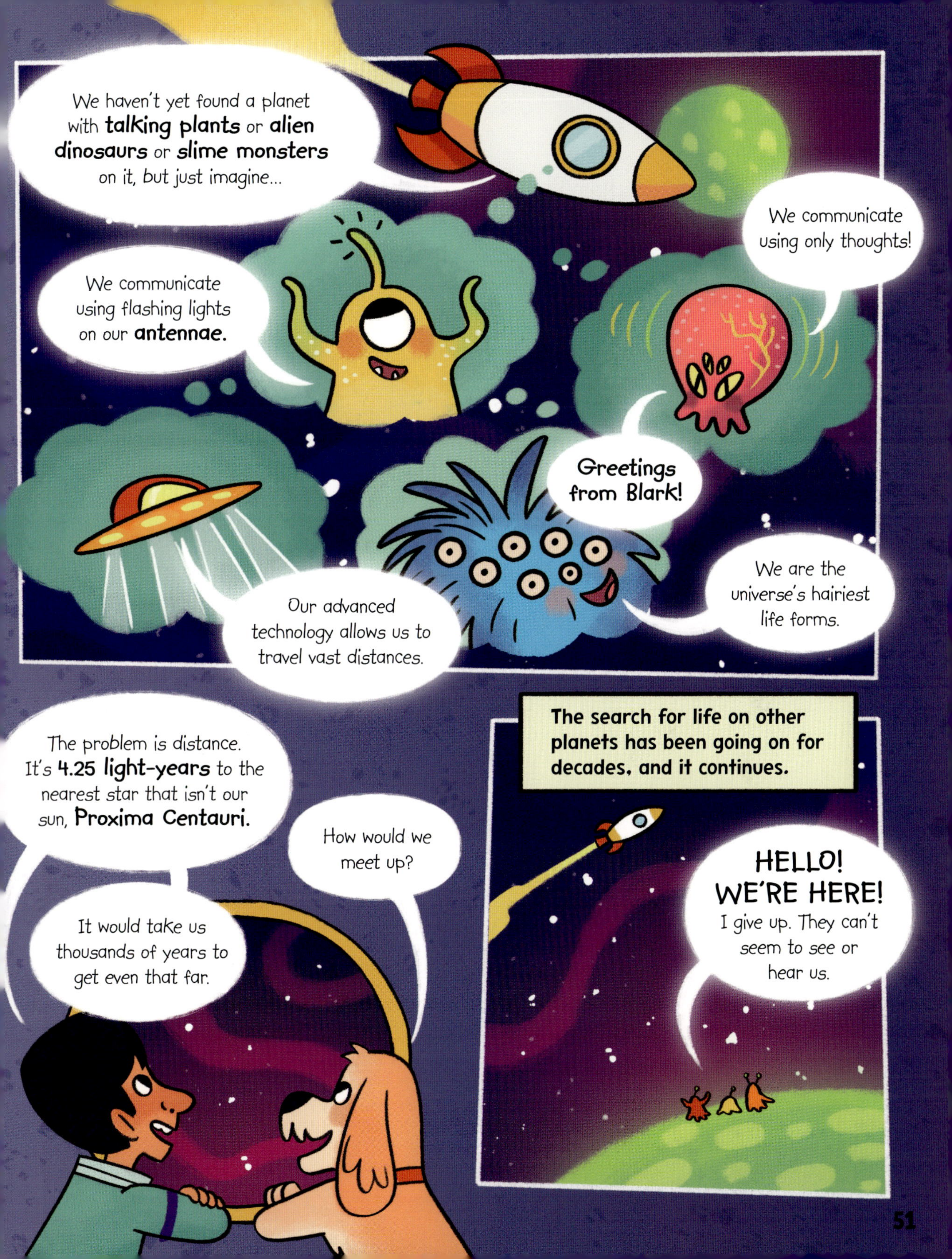

We haven't yet found a planet with **talking plants** or **alien dinosaurs** or **slime monsters** on it, but just imagine...
We communicate using flashing lights on our **antennae.**
We communicate using only thoughts!
**Greetings from Blark!**
Our advanced technology allows us to travel vast distances.
We are the universe's hairiest life forms.
The problem is distance. It's **4.25 light-years** to the nearest star that isn't our sun, **Proxima Centauri.**
How would we meet up?
It would take us thousands of years to get even that far.
**The search for life on other planets has been going on for decades, and it continues.**
HELLO! WE'RE HERE!
I give up. They can't seem to see or hear us.

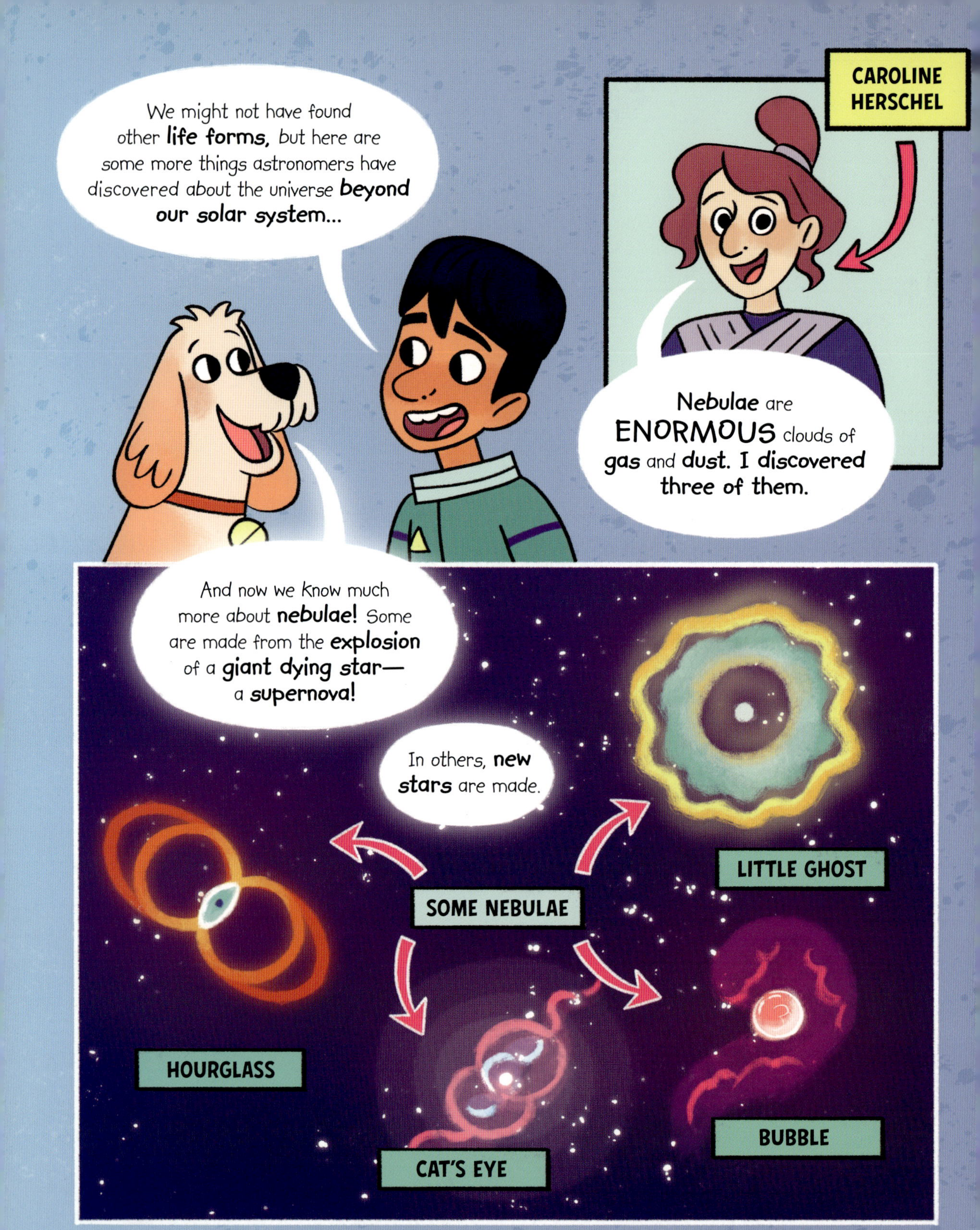
We might not have found other life forms, but here are some more things astronomers have discovered about the universe beyond our solar system...
CAROLINE HERSCHEL
Nebulae are ENORMOUS clouds of gas and dust. I discovered three of them.
And now we know much more about nebulae! Some are made from the explosion of a giant dying star—a supernova!
In others, new stars are made.
SOME NEBULAE
LITTLE GHOST
HOURGLASS
CAT'S EYE
BUBBLE

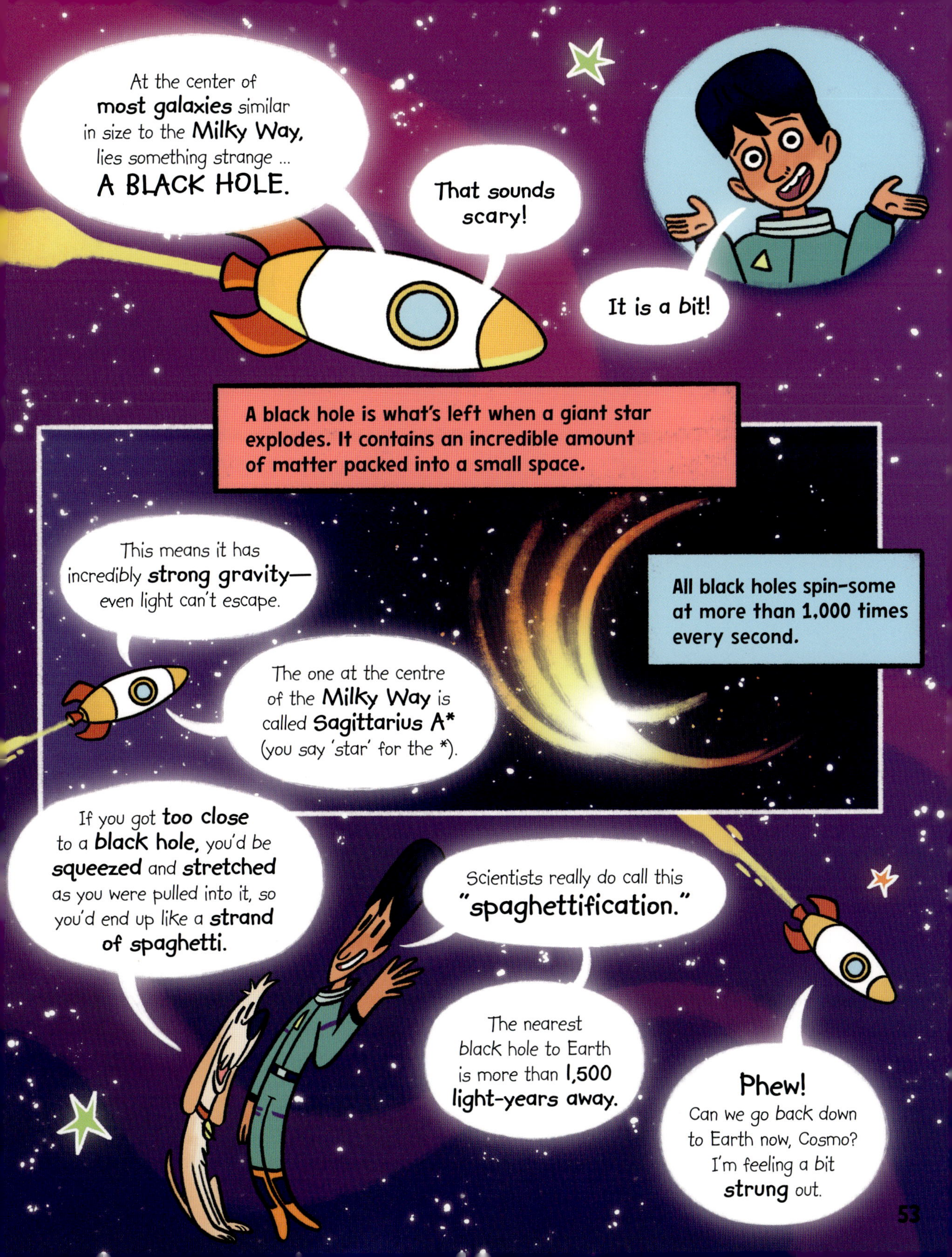
At the center of most galaxies similar in size to the Milky Way, lies something strange ... A BLACK HOLE.
That sounds scary!
It is a bit!
A black hole is what's left when a giant star explodes. It contains an incredible amount of matter packed into a small space.
This means it has incredibly strong gravity—even light can't escape.
All black holes spin–some at more than 1,000 times every second.
The one at the centre of the Milky Way is called Sagittarius A* (you say 'star' for the *).
If you got too close to a black hole, you'd be squeezed and stretched as you were pulled into it, so you'd end up like a strand of spaghetti.
Scientists really do call this "spaghettification."
The nearest black hole to Earth is more than 1,500 light-years away.
Phew! Can we go back down to Earth now, Cosmo? I'm feeling a bit strung out.

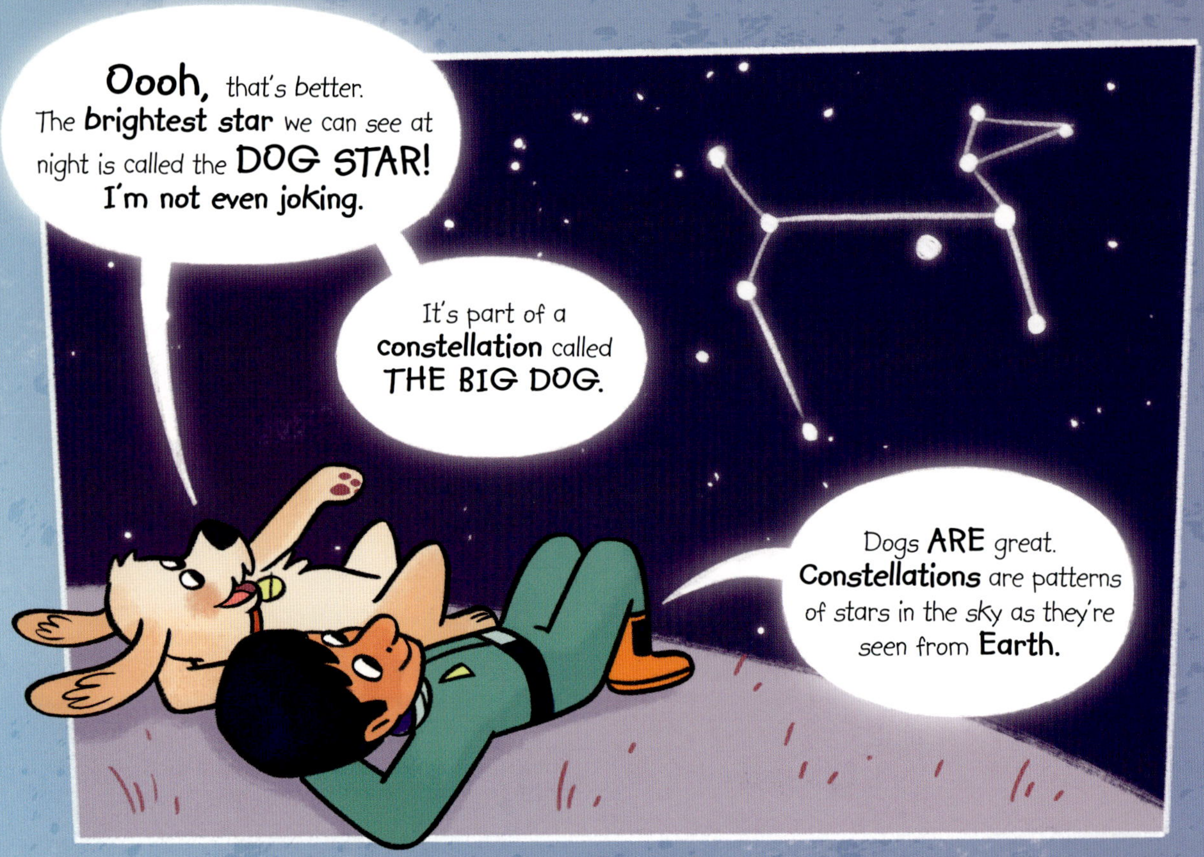
Oooh, that's better. The brightest star we can see at night is called the DOG STAR! I'm not even joking.
It's part of a constellation called THE BIG DOG.
Dogs ARE great. Constellations are patterns of stars in the sky as they're seen from Earth.

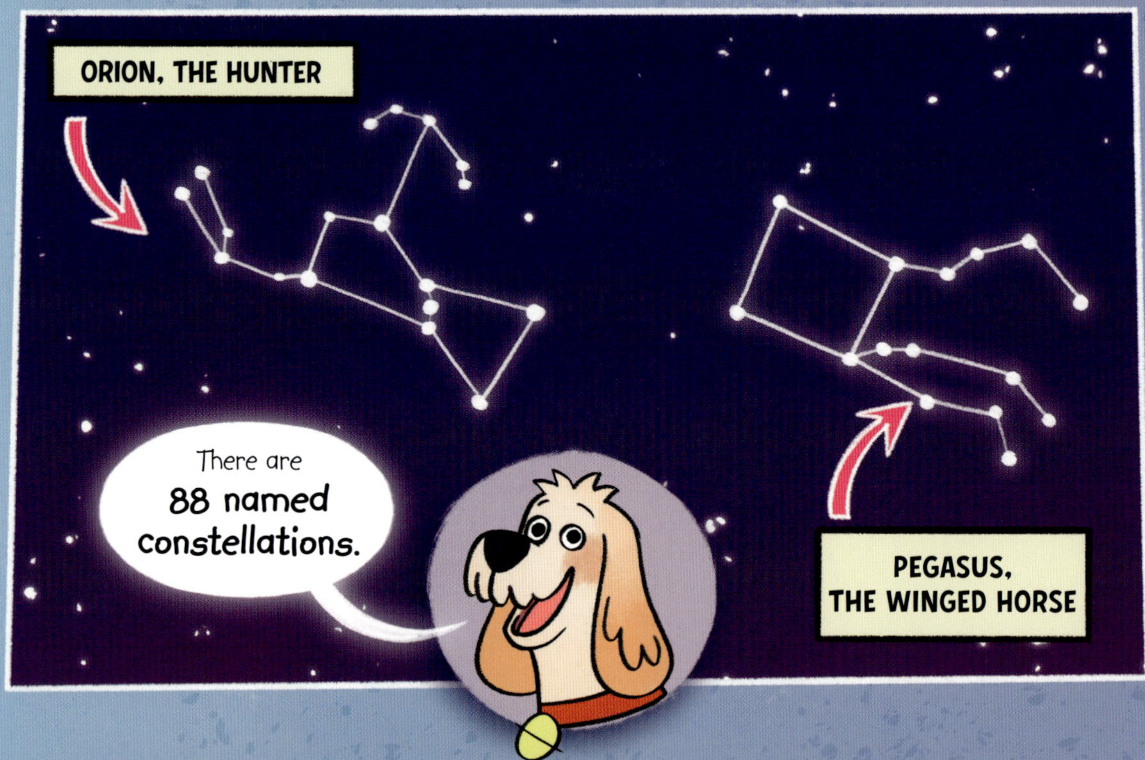
ORION, THE HUNTER
PEGASUS, THE WINGED HORSE
There are 88 named constellations.

There are different kinds of stars. And they change during their lifetime! For example...

**Red dwarfs** are the **smallest, coolest,** and **dimmest stars.** They're also the **most common**—but none of them are **bright** enough to see just with our **EYES.**

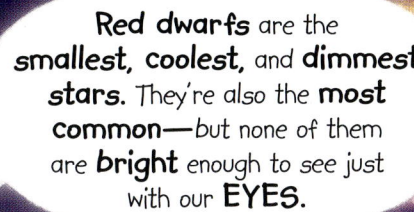

**BIGGER, hotter** stars like our **SUN** expand and become **red giants** (this will happen to our sun in billions of years' time).

The most **MASSIVE** stars explode in a **supernova,** many times brighter than the original star. Eventually they might become a **BLACK HOLE.**

**Did you know** that **stars, planets, asteroids** and that sort of thing only take up about **one percent of the universe?**

**REALLY?** What's the rest of it, then?

And another **four percent** is the **GAS** between **stars.**

**Everything** else is **DARK ENERGY** (nearly 70 percent) and **DARK MATTER** (nearly 30 percent).

It's just that ... we're not really sure **what they are.**

We're working on it though!

But there's a lot we **DO KNOW...**

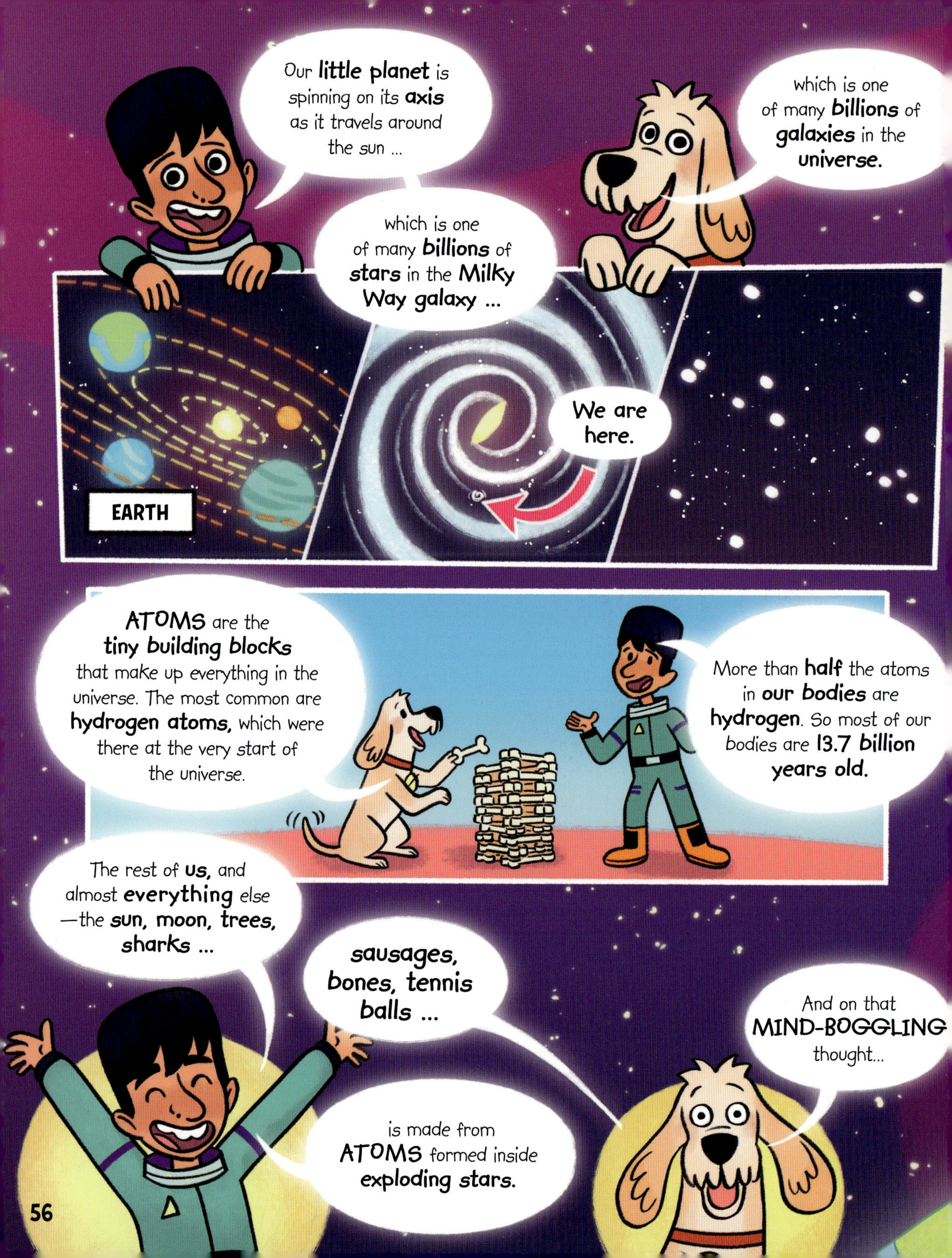

Our little planet is spinning on its axis as it travels around the sun ...
which is one of many billions of stars in the Milky Way galaxy ...
which is one of many billions of galaxies in the universe.
EARTH
We are here.
ATOMS are the tiny building blocks that make up everything in the universe. The most common are hydrogen atoms, which were there at the very start of the universe.
More than half the atoms in our bodies are hydrogen. So most of our bodies are 13.7 billion years old.
The rest of us, and almost everything else —the sun, moon, trees, sharks ...
sausages, bones, tennis balls ...
is made from ATOMS formed inside exploding stars.
And on that MIND-BOGGLING thought...

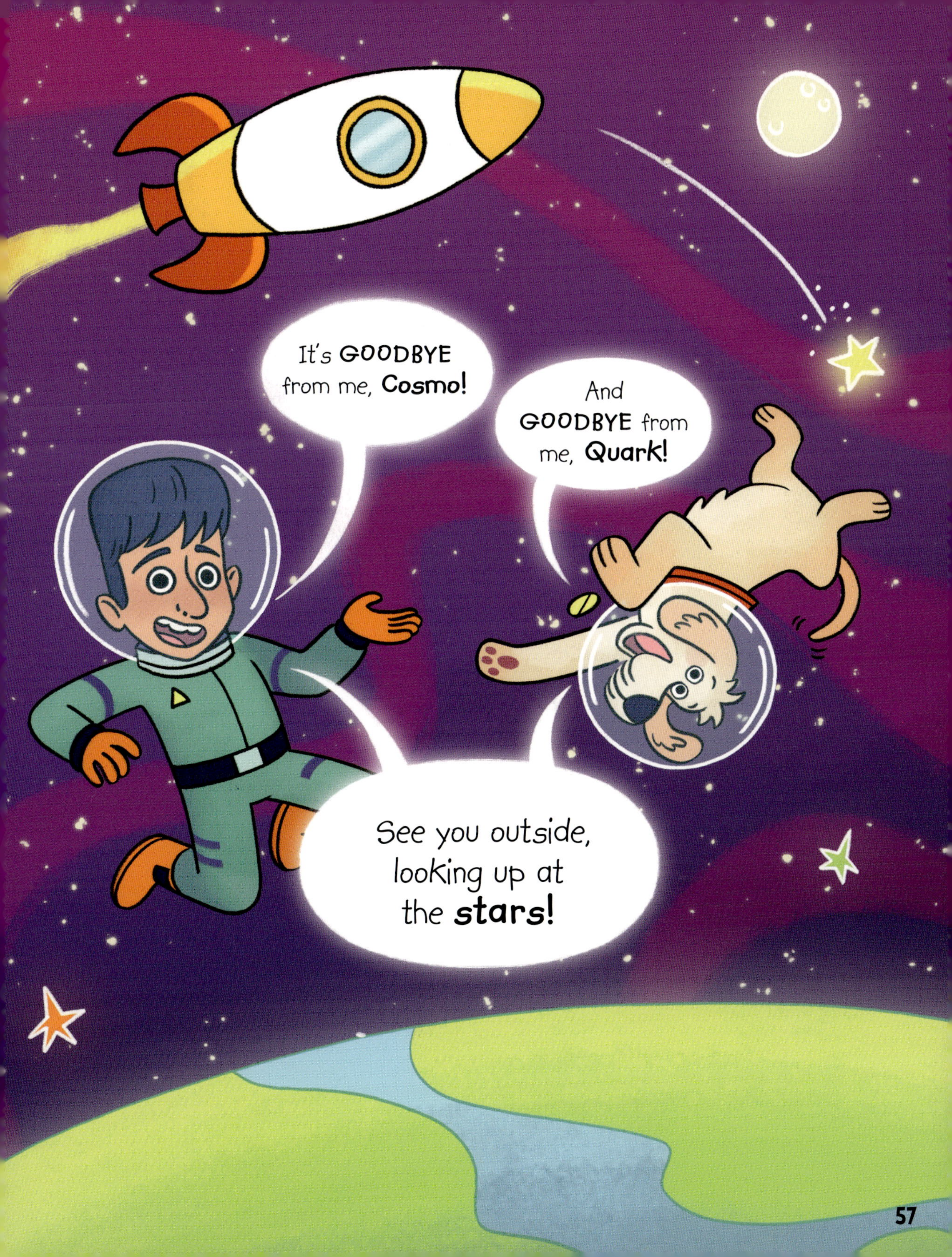
It's GOODBYE from me, Cosmo!
And GOODBYE from me, Quark!
See you outside, looking up at the stars!

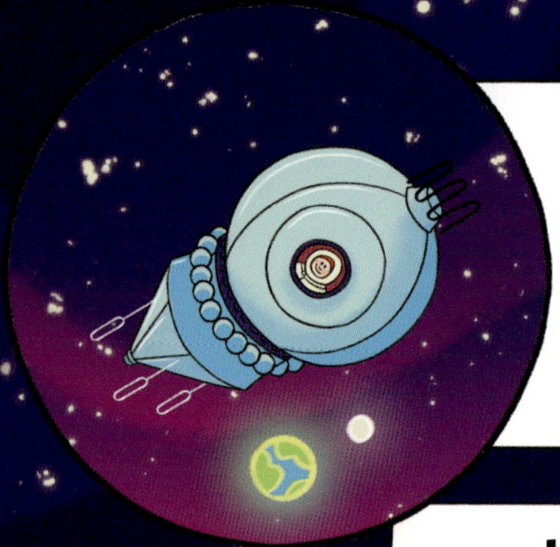

## YURI GAGARIN (1934-1968)

Soviet cosmonaut and pilot who became the first person to travel into space, and the first to orbit Earth, aboard the *Vostok 1* space capsule in 1961.

# LUNAR ASTRONAUTS

**(all are American)**

### NEIL ARMSTRONG (1930-2012)

The first person to set foot on the moon in 1969, during the Apollo 11 space flight.

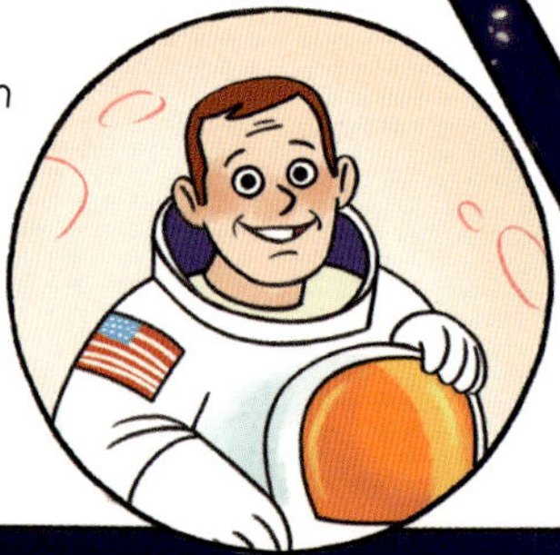

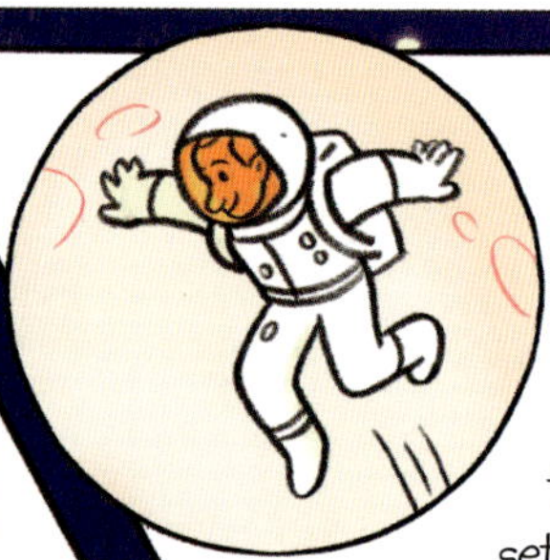

### BUZZ ALDRIN (BORN 1930)

Piloted the lunar module during the Apollo 11 spaceflight, and became the second person to set foot on the moon.

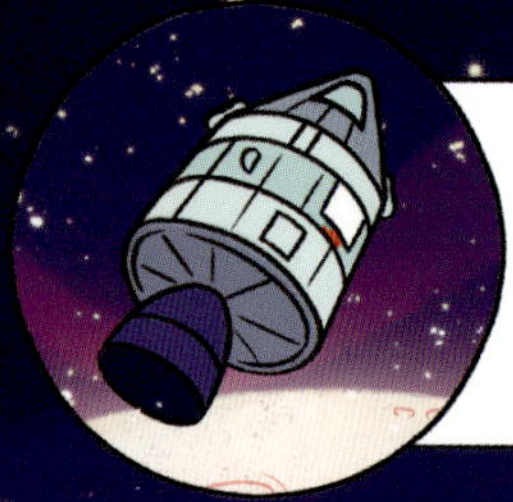

### MICHAEL COLLINS (1930-2021)

Flew the Apollo 11 command module around the moon while his crewmates, Neil Armstrong and Buzz Aldrin, landed on its surface.

### ALAN SHEPARD (1923-1998)

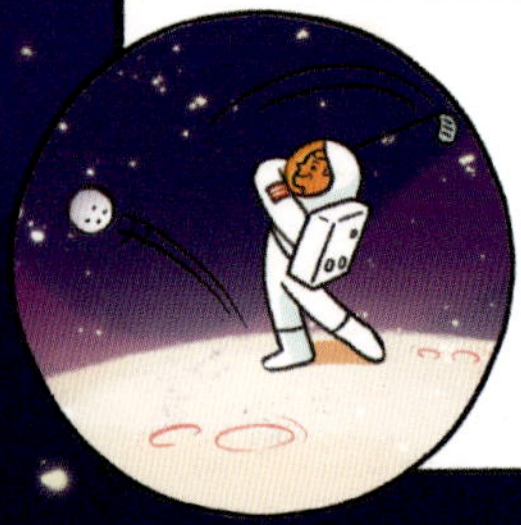

The second person to travel into space (after Yuri Gagarin), the fifth person to walk on the moon in 1971, and the only person to hit golf balls from its surface.

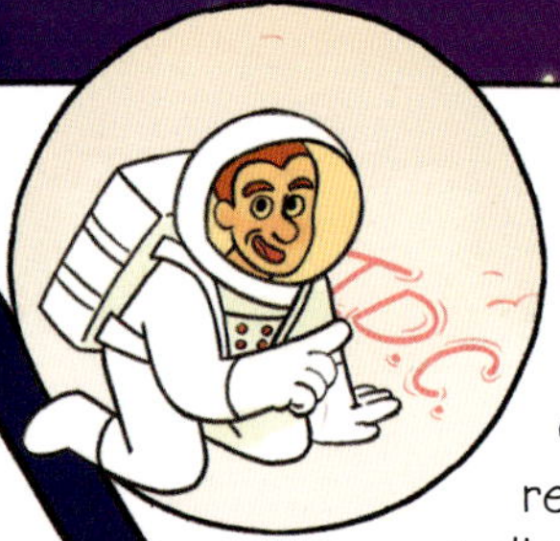

### EUGENE CERNAN (1934-2017)

The 11th (and currently the most recent) person to walk on the moon, in 1972.

## NICOLAUS COPERNICUS (1473-1543)

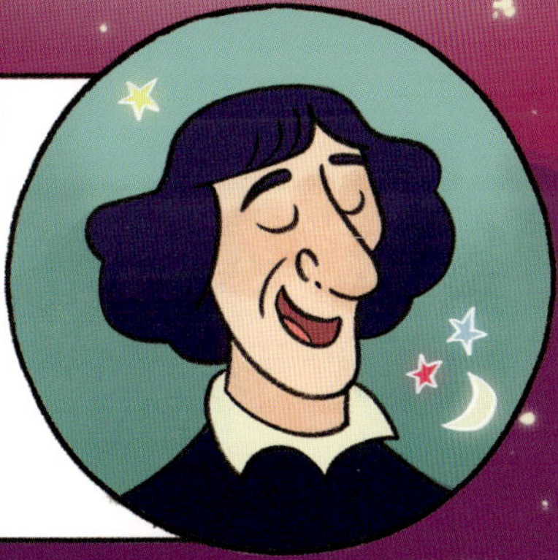

Polish mathematician and astronomer who helped prove that Earth and other planets are in orbit around the sun, contrary to popular belief at the time. His book, *On the Revolution of Heavenly Spheres*, changed science forever.

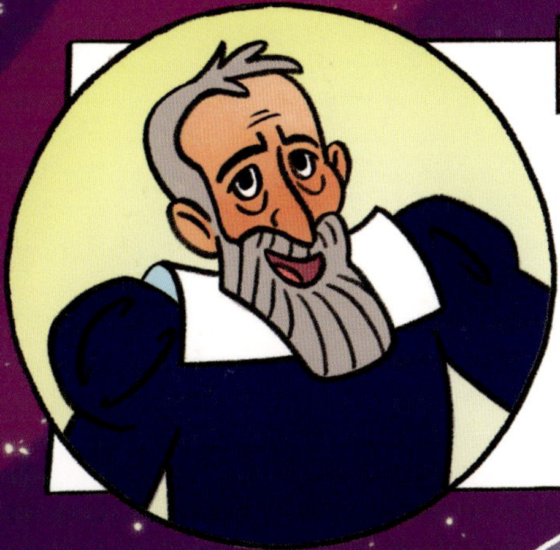

## GALILEO GALILEI (1564-1642)

Italian scientist and astronomer who built the first telescope used to study space, made many discoveries (including four of Jupiter's moons), and helped to prove Nicolaus Copernicus's theory.

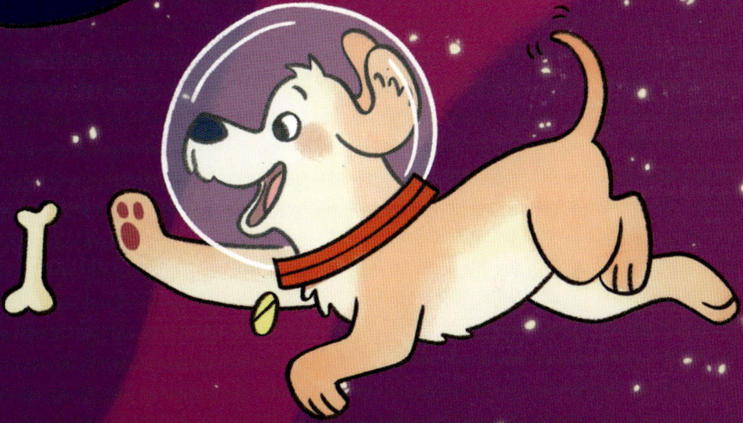

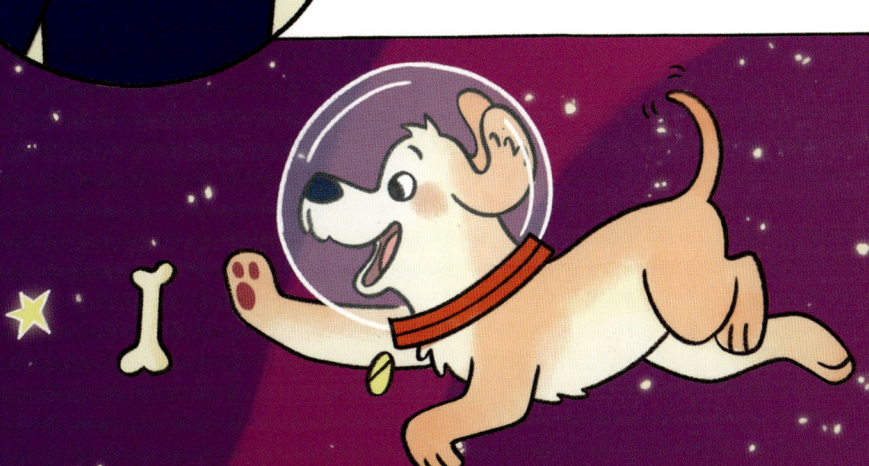

## EDMOND HALLEY (1656-1742)

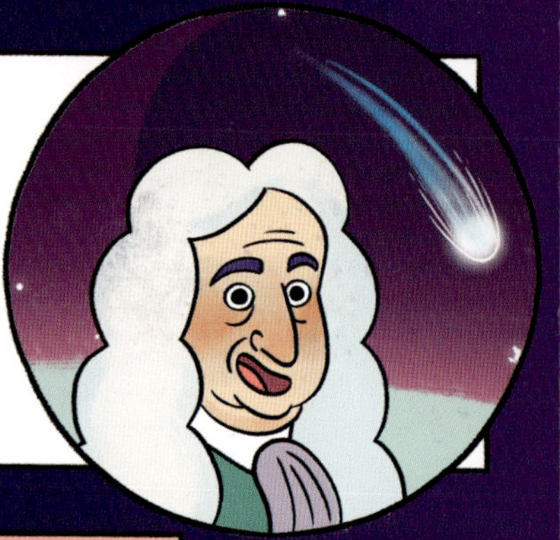

English astronomer and mathematician who calculated the orbit of a "periodic" (returning) comet he observed in 1682. The comet is now known as Halley's comet, which can be seen from Earth about once every 75 years.

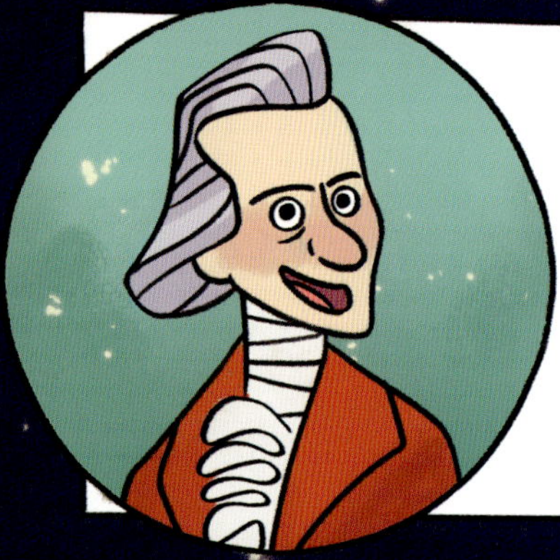

## WILLIAM HERSCHEL (1738-1822)

German-British astronomer who discovered the planet Uranus. The telescopes he made, with the help of his sister, Caroline, were the best and most powerful of the time. Together with Caroline, he spotted comets and nebulae and suggested that nebulae are made up of stars.

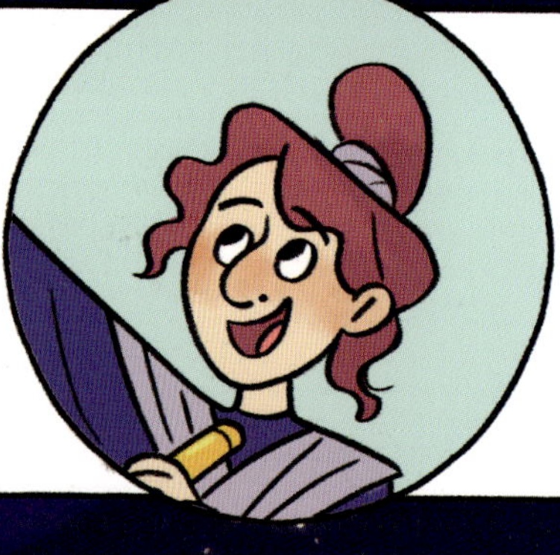

## CAROLINE HERSCHEL (1750-1848)

German-British astronomer who discovered several comets and nebulae. She was the first woman to discover a comet and the first woman to be a professional astronomer. She also contributed to the work of her brother, William Herschel.

## ALBERT EINSTEIN (1879-1955)

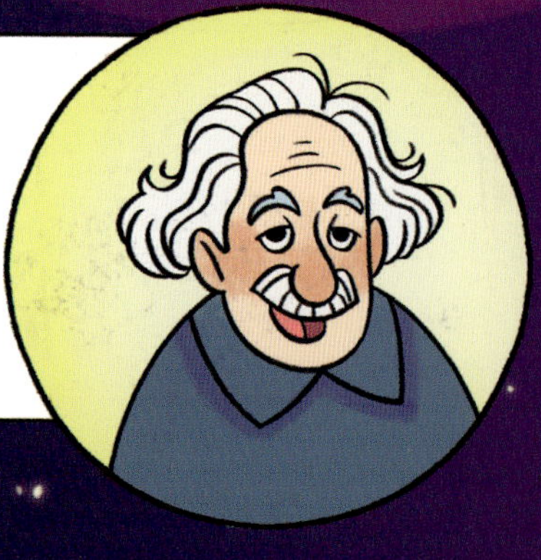

Physicist who made many groundbreaking discoveries about the universe and the nature of gravity. His two most famous works are his *Special* and *General Theories of Relativity*.

## JAN OORT (1900-1992)

Dutch astronomer who calculated the position of our sun within the Milky Way galaxy, and that the Milky Way rotates. He came up with the theory that the solar system is surrounded by an enormous cloud of icy, comet-like objects, which is now known as the Oort Cloud.

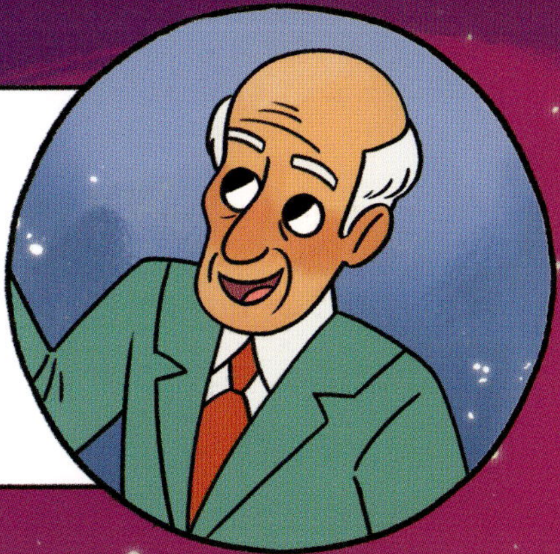

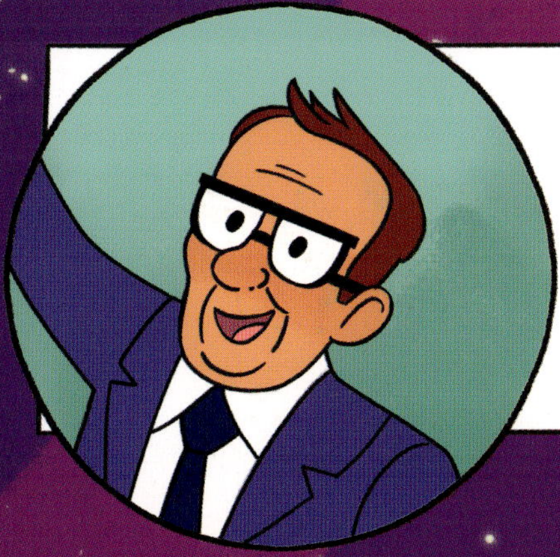

## GERARD KUIPER (1905-1973)

Dutch-American astronomer who discovered moons of Uranus and Neptune. In 1951, he suggested the existence of a disk-shaped region of objects outside Neptune's orbit, the area that's now known as the Kuiper Belt.

## NATALIE BATALHA (born 1966)

American astronomer who led NASA's Kepler mission, which discovered more than 2,700 exoplanets. Her work focuses on exoplanets and the search for life beyond our solar system.

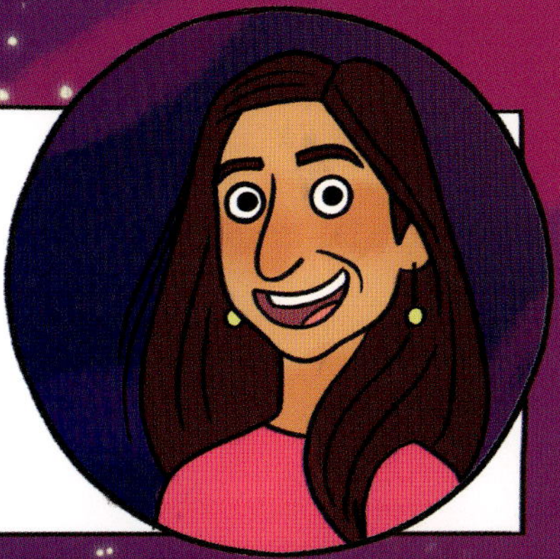

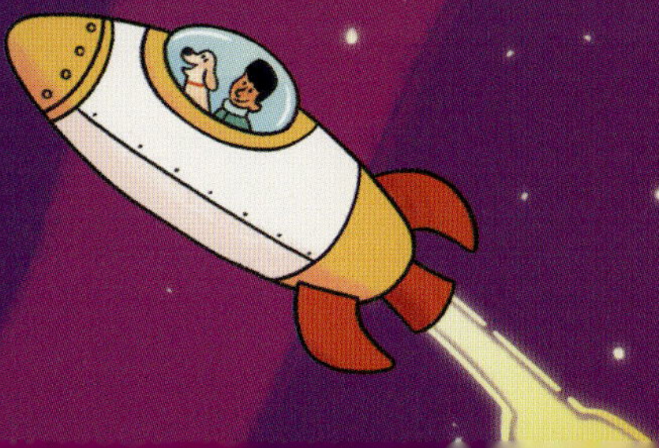

# GLOSSARY

**asteroid:** small, rocky object in orbit around the sun

**astronaut:** someone who has been trained to travel into space (cosmonauts are astronauts from Russia or the Soviet Union

**astronomer:** someone who studies stars, planets, and other objects in space

**black hole:** extremely dense object spinning in space with such strong gravity that nothing can escape from it—not even light

**comet:** large object made of ice and dust in orbit around the sun. Comets, with their long, streaming tails, can sometimes be seen from Earth

**constellation:** pattern of stars as seen from Earth

**dwarf planet:** large, roundish object in orbit around the sun

**exoplanet:** planet outside of our solar system

**galaxy:** group of thousands, millions, or billions of stars, and accompanying planets, asteroids, etc., held together by gravity

**gravity:** invisible force pulling objects toward one another, which keeps us on the ground, and also keeps planets in orbit around the sun

**light-year:** distance light travels in one year

**meteor:** chunk of rock and other material that burns up in Earth's atmosphere and can sometimes be seen streaking across the sky

**meteorite:** chunk of rock and other material that doesn't completely burn up as it passes through the atmosphere, and falls to Earth

**moon:** Earth's only natural satellite; other moons orbit other objects in our solar system

**orbit:** the path of an object around another object in space

**nebula:** enormous cloud of dust and gas in space (plural nebulae)

**planet:** spherical object in orbit around a star that has no other similar objects close to its orbit

**satellite:** object in orbit around a larger object

**solar system:** our sun and everything in orbit around it, including planets, asteroids, and comets

**star:** shining ball of extremely hot, burning gas. Stars come in different colors and sizes

**sun:** star at the center of our solar system

**supernova:** explosion that destroys a massive star

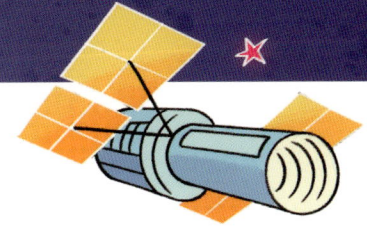

# INDEX

Adams, John Couch .................................. 41
Aldrin, Buzz ........................................... 17, 58
aliens ................................................... 50-51
animals in space ..................................... 18-19
Apollo 11 ........................................... 16-17, 58
Armstrong, Neil ..................................... 16, 58
Asteroid Belt ........................................ 42-43
asteroids ................................... 30, 36, 42-43
astronauts ............. 16-17, 19, 22-23, 25, 58
astronomers ................................. 59, 60, 61
atoms ..................................................... 56

Batalha, Natalie ................................... 50, 61
birthdays ................................................. 10
black holes ..................................... 5, 53, 55

Ceres ...................................................... 43
Cernan, Eugene .................................. 17, 58
Collins, Michael ................................... 17, 58
comets .............................. 45, 46-47, 60, 61
constellations ......................................... 54
Copernicus, Nicolaus .......................... 13, 59
cosmonauts ........................................ 24, 58
craters ............................................... 12, 48

dark energy ............................................ 55
dark matter ............................................ 55
days ............................................. 10, 32-41
dinosaurs ............................................... 29
dog biscuits ......................................... 5, 26
dwarf planets ....................... 30, 42, 43, 44

Earth .................... 6, 8, 9, 10-11, 30, 34, 56
Einstein, Albert .................................. 49, 60
exoplanets ......................................... 50, 61

Gagarin, Yuri .................................. 24, 29, 58
galaxies ............................... 48-49, 50, 56, 61
Galileo Galilei .............................. 37, 48, 59
Galle, Johann Gottfried .......................... 41
Ganymede .............................................. 37
gas giants ........................................... 36-39
golf .......................................... 5, 17, 58
gravity ............................... 13, 20, 26, 53, 60

Halley, Edmond .................................. 46, 60
Herschel, Caroline ............................ 47, 52, 60
Herschel, William ............................ 40, 47, 60

International Space Station ............. 22-23

Jupiter ...................... 31, 36-37, 39, 42, 48

Kuiper Belt ......................................... 44, 46
Kuiper, Gerard .................................... 44, 61

Le Verrier, Urbain ................................... 41

light-years ............................................. 49
living in space ................................... 26-27

# INDEX (contd)

Mars .................................... 30, 35, 42
Mercury ........................ 30, 32, 35, 37
meteors ...................................... 28
meteorites .................................. 29
meteoroids ................................. 28
Milky Way ............ 15, 48, 49, 53, 56, 61
moon ........................ 5, 6, 12-17, 20, 34
moons ............................ 35, 36, 37, 38, 48

NASA ........................................ 17, 61
nebulae .................................... 52, 60
Neptune ...................... 31, 39, 41, 44, 61
North Pole .................................. 11

Oort Cloud ................................ 45, 46
Oort, Jan .................................. 45, 61
orbits .................. 9, 10, 20, 26, 30-31, 36

phases of the moon .................. 14-15
planets ........................ 30-41, 49, 50, 56

rings ........................................ 38, 39
rockets .................................... 16, 24

satellites .................................. 20-23
Saturn ...................................... 31, 38-39
seasons .................................... 10-11,
Shepard, Alan ............................ 17, 58
solar system ............................ 30-46
South Pole ................................ 11
spacesuits ................................ 25
spaghettification ...................... 55
stars ............................ 7, 48, 49, 52, 53,
                                           54-55, 56, 57
sun .................................... 6, 8-11, 30
supernova ................................ 52, 55

telescopes .............. 37, 40, 47, 48, 49, 60
Titan ........................................ 38

Uranus .................................. 31, 39, 40, 61

Venus ...................................... 30, 33

years ...................................... 10, 32-41

64